CULTURES OF CHANGE:

Recovery and Relapse Prevention for Dually Diagnosed and Addicted Adolescents

Janice E. Gabe, MSW, CCSW, NCACII

Published by
Professional Resource Publications
P.O. Box 501485
Indianapolis, IN 46256

ISBN: 0-9639023-0-X

Publisher's Cataloging-in-Publication Data

Layout and cover design by *WordWorks Publishing*.
Printed in the United States

DEDICATION

To my husband, Steve, and my precious son, Kyle.
To the folks, Sharon, Stan, Fran and Harold.

To recovering adolescents everywhere who have the courage to face their addiction and to the special adults who have helped them along the way.

ACKNOWLEDGEMENTS

I want to extend my thanks to the following treatment programs who participated in the research on adolescent relapse:

Fairbanks Hospital, Indianapolis, Indiana

Rosecrance Center, Rockford, Illinois

Hartview Center, Mandan, North Dakota

Amethyst, Charlotte, North Carolina

Youth and Shelter Services, Ames, Iowa

Rimrock Foundation, Billings, Montana

Brighton Hospital, Brighton, Michigan

The Strong One

Darkness crept upon us
There was eternal night
It crept into every heart
And shut out all the lights
Pain and death surrounding
Misery and fear
Each brings us close
To the end we fear is near
But one heart wouldn't listen
It held onto the sun
I won't give up on life just yet
There's work now to be done
One lonely soul held onto faith
So it could teach the world to care
In the hope that love in every heart
Won't always be so rare.

By Kimberly

CONTENTS

INTRODUCTION

The incidence of relapse among addicted and dually-diagnosed adolescents is one of the most critical issues facing professionals who work with teenagers and their families. As I travel around the country, I hear the same comments over and over—"Everyone told us about identification, intervention and referral, but no one told us about relapse." The fact that many teens return to use following a treatment experience has left professionals who work with teens feeling that treatment has been unsuccessful. Many individuals who work in schools, probation departments, and outpatient counseling clinics worked diligently to establish systems that would identify substance-abusing youth and make treatment available. These same individuals are now feeling discouraged because of what they view as poor treatment outcomes.

I recently saw a seventeen-year-old-adolescent who was in residential care at a treatment center where I consult. I had seen her on an outpatient basis when she was twelve years old. She proceeded to tell me that the only reason she was in treatment was because her older sister was the perfect child and had not been in treatment. When I asked her to elaborate on this point, she indicated that several of her friends had older brothers and sisters who had been in drug rehabilitation or in psychiatric programs. Since very few of these young people stayed clean or significantly improved their level of functioning after treatment, their parents had concluded that treatment did not work and had decided to ignore the drug use and problem behavior when it surfaced in the younger siblings in the family. This seventeen-year-old unknowingly described a key issue for the adolescent treatment community.

For years, individuals have not understood the phenomenon of adolescent relapse. We have not received useful information about it, we have not thoroughly examined our attitudes about it and we have not addressed it effectively. Many of us have felt helpless as professionals when the teens we work with return to chemical use. In response to this helpless feeling, we have done things which have been counterproductive. During the early 1980's we did not know how to address this issue, so we rationalized by making comments such as, "Sometimes it takes teens five or six times through treatment to get a grasp on recovery." We set up a revolving door of treatment which resulted in teens going from one treatment program to the next and still not remaining free of chemicals. We tried to take firm stands in an effort to force kids to stay clean.

I used the "firm stand" approach early in my career by telling members of the aftercare group which I led that if they relapsed three times, they would be out of group. The teens were not stupid; they would talk about the first two relapses and would lie about the rest. Since I had created an environment that made it difficult for them to be honest about their use, they could not talk about their struggles in recovery, and the group was powerless to help them. As a result, many of them were lost.

During the late 1980's and moving into the 1990's, we have responded to our frustration at adolescent relapse by ignoring substance abuse as a primary issue. In many parts of the country, we are seeing the re-emergence of the interpretation of adolescent drug use as a symptom of a psychiatric disorder. Unfortunately, the attempt to ignore adolescent addiction or to treat it as a psychiatric disorder has done nothing to reduce the rate of adolescent relapse.

In thirteen years of working with addicted and dually-diagnosed youth, I have learned that adolescents can and do recover. I know hundreds of young people who are in strong recovery programs that began during their adolescence. I have also learned that in order to be effective in working with these young people, we have to re-examine our attitude about and our approach to adolescent treatment and adolescent relapse prevention.

The purpose of this book is to challenge us to understand that by re-examining our approach to addicted and dually-diagnosed teens in early recovery, we will be able to help teens move past relapse into recovery. We will also be able to utilize relapse as a powerful clinical tool in our work with teens and their families. However, to move in this direction, we must realize that we have to challenge and question many of the concepts about treatment which we have held sacred. Many of these wisdoms are important in treating adults, but are not valid when treating teens. As long as we continue to hold rigidly to these "truths," we will be ineffective in working with adolescents. This book is intended to serve as a practical guide to understanding issues specific to treatment and relapse prevention for adolescents who have a primary diagnosis of addiction as well as addicted adolescents who have a coexisting psychiatric diagnosis. It will explore the dimension of adolescent relapse; identify adolescent specific relapse dynamics, signs, and symptoms; discuss specific relapse prevention techniques; outline a relapse intervention process and explore the special treatment needs of adolescents who have relapsed. In addition, this book will provide a framework for understanding adolescent involvement in negative subcultures as part of their dysfunction and the importance of creating cultures of change for our young people. Finally, this book will provide a framework for motivating families to recover.

CHAPTER

1

BASIC ASSUMPTIONS
AND DEFINITIONS

There are several basic assumptions and definitions which must be understood before proceeding. The first order of business is to define important terms. Because we lack definitions of key terms, we often have trouble communicating our ideas.

RECOVERY

We must first clarify what we mean when we use the word "recovery." When treatment professionals are asked what types of recovery rates we expect, a frequent response is the question, "What do you mean by recovery?"

For the purpose of this book, we will define recovery in the following way:

"Recovery is the ongoing process of improving one's level of functioning while striving to maintain abstinence from mood altering chemicals."

Let's examine key concepts of this definition. "Ongoing process" tells us that recovery is not an event that takes place while the young person is in the treatment center. Rather, it is something that they struggle with in day-to-day life. Recovery is something that is new and different to the young person.

Because it is new, it is not something they will achieve without great difficulty. It is not something they will achieve instantly and it is not something they will accomplish without making many mistakes in the process. While most professionals agree that recovery is a process, we have failed to respect the process. As professionals, we have often been narrowly focused on a small part of the process known as primary treatment. We have failed to focus on what comes before primary treatment and what comes after it. This narrow focus has contributed to the relapse rates for teens. If we truly believe that staying clean and sober is a process, then we must acknowledge that getting clean and sober is part of the process. Tammy Bell has written extensively on the subject of pretreatment (Bell, 1990). Bell makes a critical point that one of the important tasks of adolescent treatment professionals is to utilize pretreatment as a way to motivate and prepare young people to enter into an abstinence-based recovery mode.

"Improving one's level of functioning" is an important concept in this definition. The key word is improving. The true measure of success is determined not by examining where the young person is in recovery, but by examining the distance they have traveled. If the young person has a long history of school absences prior to treatment, and his attendance improves in recovery, that is an indication that the teen is moving forward in recovery. That does not mean his attendance at school must be perfect in order for his recovery to be solid. Similarly, if teens are fighting less with their families, participating in fewer illegal activities, making better grades, trying to make new friends, and are more emotionally or behaviorally stable, these are all indications of recovery. Unfortunately, we frequently expect perfection, not progress, in these areas.

Oddly enough, when working with adults who are addicted, we have few expectations of them during the early months of recovery. Adults frequently quit their jobs, abdicate parental responsibility, and behave in ways that are irresponsible and immature during the early months in recovery. We frequently ignore these behaviors and remind ourselves that at least they are not drinking and that, after all, is the important thing. However, when teens struggle and display behaviors that are immature and irresponsible in recovery, we quickly confront them on not working their programs and we begin to think they have not learned anything in treatment. I am not suggesting that we should ignore behavioral problems that surface with teens in recovery, but I am suggesting that we become more realistic in our expectations for these teens.

"Striving to maintain abstinence from mood-altering chemicals" reminds us that as long as the teens are making a sincere effort to remain chemically free, they are engaged in the recovery process. While they are striving toward abstinence, most teens will return to isolated incidents of drug use somewhere along the way. They will make mistakes in their recovery. As long as teens are sincerely striving to maintain abstinence, we should strive to help them in this process.

RELAPSE AND SLIPS

The terms "relapse" and "slips" also need to be discussed in this chapter.

Slips are defined as isolated incidents of use experienced by adolescents whose goal is abstinence.

When working with teens, it is important to distinguish between slips and relapses. It is safe to assume that the majority of teens will experience slips during their recovery. If we become more skilled at dealing with slips, relapses can be prevented. Slips do not mean treatment failure. Slips need to be addressed as a clinical issue which will inevitably surface in working with addicted teens. It is our attitude about slips which will determine, to a large extent, whether or not the slips will be therapeutic for the teens. Having rules against slips and being intolerant of them will not stop them from occurring. This attitude will only stop them from being discussed. If they are not discussed, the young person cannot be helped with them. When I present this idea to professionals, they frequently state, "Sounds like you are just giving the kids permission to go out and use again."

My experience with teens has taught me that they do not need my permission to use again. Many teens in recovery have been slipping for years without my permission. As I once heard Tammy Bell point out, on one hand we tell the adolescents that they have a progressive, chronic disease called chemical dependency. Like all chronic diseases, relapse or slips are a reality. On the other hand, we respond to relapse in teens punitively, as if we are dealing with a behavior problem.

The reality, whether we like it or not, is that most teens will slip in recovery. Our choices are to ignore this reality and fail when trying to work with them, or to accept the reality and become more skilled in working with this issue.

Relapse is defined as a decision to return to the use of mood-altering chemicals. This decision inevitably results in a return to old drug use patterns and old drug use behaviors.

Adolescents in relapse are not striving to maintain abstinence. They have made a conscious decision not to continue in the recovery process. They may acknowledge this decision to you openly, or they may demonstrate it by what they do. For example, teens in relapse may talk about their use and indicate they want to get back on track in their recovery, but they do not make any effort to follow through on their plans to do so. This is an indication that the adolescent has made a decision not to continue in recovery.

When working with teens, it is important to assess whether the teen is in relapse or whether the teen is experiencing slips. Teens who are experiencing slips but are making an effort to do better, are teens who are in recovery. Interventions for teens in recovery are different than interventions for teens who are in total relapse.

FOUR CATEGORIES OF
POST TREATMENT ADOLESCENTS

Post treatment teens usually fall into one of four categories. The first category is referred to as the roller coaster up and looks like this:

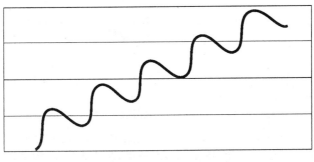

Roller Coaster Up

This diagram is a reflection of what recovery truly looks like for teens. The Jelnick curve for teens does not accurately depict adolescent recovery because it implies a relatively smooth and steady growth in recovery. In reality, the road to recovery for teens is very rocky and is filled with many ups and downs.

This is due in part to the very nature of adolescents. The roller coaster consists of times when the adolescent appears to be doing well in recovery (high points on the roller coaster) followed by times when the adolescent does very poorly (low points on the roller coaster). Low points on the roller coaster may consist of episodic and isolated incidents of use (slips) or other dysfunctional behavior. For example, addicted teens may not be using, but they may make poor choices which create problems for them in their life. These poor choices commonly consist of behaviors such as ignoring curfew, skipping school, staying out all night, lying to parents about what they are doing, or refusing to address their psychiatric treatment issues. These behaviors are frustrating for counselors to deal with, but are the very behaviors which need to be addressed in early recovery. As recovery continues, the periods of use or dysfunctional behavior become less and less frequent.

The second category of post treatment teens is called the roller coaster down and looks like this:

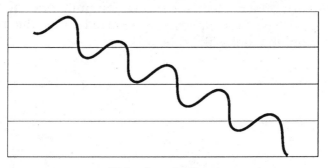

Roller Coaster Down

Teens in this category start out doing well in recovery; however, the incidents of use and dysfunctional behavior become increasingly more frequent. The therapist feels he is losing ground with this patient and that the patient is slipping further and further into a relapse dynamic. These teens may slip into total relapse or they may quite unexpectedly turn things around and regain ground in their recovery.

The third category of post treatment adolescents are teens who are on the toboggan ride down which looks like this:

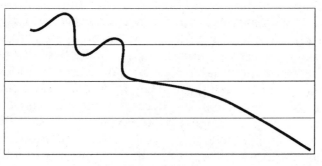

Toboggan Ride Down

These are teens who leave treatment and do well for a short period of time, but quickly loose ground and slip into relapse.

The final category of teens are adolescents who never joined the party in the first place (or never left the party). These teens look like this:

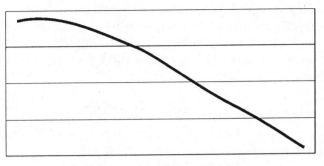

Kids Who Never Joined The Party

These teens are discharged from treatment and quickly experience a return to old drug using behaviors. It is my opinion that about twenty-five per cent of the teens who leave treatment fall into this category. These are teens who never engaged in the treatment process. They have no intentions of staying clean and sober because they are thoroughly convinced that their chemical use is not a problem for them. They have not completed the basic pretreatment task of acknowledging that the problems in their life are related to chemicals and that they cannot control their lives as long as they are actively using. These are teens who are frequently referred to long-term treatment, but these teens are poor candidates for long-term treatment. Their denial is so intense that it cannot be penetrated while they are in an inpatient treatment environment.

Long-term treatment is best saved for teens who have some level of motivation for recovery but whose living situations make recovery difficult for them. Teens who have not joined the party in the first place will likely complete long-term treatment only to relapse as soon as they return to the community. These teens need to be allowed the opportunity to return home and experience further pain and negative consequences as a result of their use. These teens do not belong in aftercare or school-based recovery groups because they are not interested in recovery. It is more appropriate to switch to a relapse intervention mode which is described in later chapters in this book.

When working with teens, I often describe these four categories to them. While kids who are struggling may be resistant to looking at "relapse behavior" because they are not using, they are more likely to admit they are on the roller coaster down and will frequently asked what they can do to change this situation.

BASIC ASSUMPTIONS

Before we continue, it is important to cover some basic assumptions about adolescent relapse.

ASSUMPTION #1:
Slips are frequently part of the recovery process for teens.

Many of us who have worked with addicted teens know hundreds of teens in recovery. Most of these teens did not grow and stabilize in their recovery without making mistakes and experiencing isolated or periodic return to the use of chemicals. I frequently tell teens that the goal for them is abstinence; however, slips can be detours in recovery or they can be dead-end streets. What happens as a result of the slip depends on how the teen and the counselor handle it. One should never tell an adolescent, "If you slip, you have to begin all over again."

First of all, this is not true. Their progress and gains have not been lost due to the slip. Secondly, adolescents are very concrete creatures who live in the present. If they are told this, many of them will simply feel defeated and give up on recovery.

Slips do not have to result in a complete relapse on the part of the teen. Professionals who work with teens need to be competent and comfortable in addressing slips. One of the common wisdoms we identify in adult treatment is that if you have not had three months of continuous clean time, you have not had recovery, and therefore have not relapsed. With teens, this statement does not hold true. Teens in early recovery may improve all areas of functioning, be attending meetings, and following all aftercare recommendations. In the midst of all this, largely due to the impulsiveness of adolescents, they may use. This means they have made a mistake in their recovery; it does not mean that recovery has not or is not happening.

ASSUMPTION #2:
Teens who relapse have
special treatment needs.

They are teens with dual diagnosis, impulse control problems, parental addiction and dysfunction, and unresolved grief and trauma such as sexual and physical abuse and numerous loss issues. Although their addiction is a primary disease, these other issues are closely tied with their use and certainly interfere with long-term recovery. These teens, by virtue of the fact they are relapsing, are telling us that they have special treatments needs. When we send these teens back through the same type of treatment over and over without addressing their special needs or without doing significant relapse prevention work, our message to them is very clear. It is a message that tells them they are failing. It is a message that clearly says to them, "You stupid shit, you're not doing it right."

In reality, it is not necessarily the teen who is failing, it is frequently the treatment professional who sticks rigidly to a standard treatment regimen regardless of whether or not this regimen is effective with this teen. We have long recognized special needs for relapsed adults and have done special programming for them. It is time that the same be done for teens. We will focus on special programming needs for these patients in a later chapter in this book.

ASSUMPTION #3:
Adolescent relapse behavior
is not to be confused with
normal adolescent behavior.

Adolescents have several developmental tasks that they need to accomplish. These tasks include the development of critical thinking; development of psychosexual identity;

21

separation and individuation from parents by asserting independence in music, dress and opinions; testing behavioral limits with authority figures; and establishing personal boundaries. These tasks make working with teens a challenge.

When we are met with challenges, we frequently respond by developing rules against the behavior that makes us uncomfortable. For example, teenage romance is often difficult for adults to deal with because of its level of intensity. We tell teens not to engage in romantic relationships until they have been clean for a year. We do this because the emotional intensity of these relationships may result in teens slipping. However, teens cannot accomplish an important developmental task if they do not participate in these romantic relationships.

It is better that we respect where the teens are developmentally and teach them healthy ways to handle romantic relationships than to ignore the issue by telling them not to engage in relationships. Similarly, teens who are practicing skills of critical thinking or expressing their individuality by questioning our direction or by dressing in ways that make us uncomfortable, are labeled as resistant. This is not necessarily resistance, it is adolescence. These behaviors are not always signs of relapse, but are sometimes signs of teens struggling to grow up. We cannot become so rigid in setting rules for recovery that we block their avenues for accomplishing their adolescent developmental tasks.

ASSUMPTION #4:
Recovery is a
developmental process.

The developmental process of recovery as defined by Gorski (Gorski, 1986) indicates that recovery begins with patients learning basic recovery related tasks which serve as building blocks.

As recovery continues, the tasks become increasingly more complex. This definition requires that we evaluate our expectations of teens early in recovery. Frequently, we expect teens in early recovery to be accomplishing tasks that they are not ready to tackle until late recovery. We also expect them to do things that are difficult for many healthy, non-addicted teens.

This list of expectations includes: identify and discuss their feelings, utilize problem solving skills, obey the rules at home, communicate with their parents, make new friends, go to school and attend their classes, learn to assert themselves, learn confidence and improve self-esteem, make lifestyle changes, improve their attitude towards authority figures, follow their aftercare plan, make good decisions, take responsibility for their recovery, learn to utilize a Higher Power, etc., etc. Often, our unspoken expectation is that if the teens do not accomplish these things, then treatment has not been successful.

While we certainly hope the teen will improve in these areas as he/she matures in recovery, it is unrealistic to expect that the teen will do these things early in recovery. In fact, we would not expect adults to be able to accomplish all these tasks early in recovery. As we review this list, we recognize that it is unrealistic; however, it is often what we expect. When teens receive the message that this is what you have to do to be a recovering young person, they become overwhelmed and feel like giving up. Indeed, any adolescent would feel that way when encountered with such a list of expectations.

ASSUMPTION #5:
We cannot confuse normal adolescent behavior with relapse behavior and we cannot use recovery as an excuse to avoid dealing with adolescent developmental tasks.

We frequently refer to the fact that addicted teens are emotionally and socially arrested from a developmental point of view.

Few professionals disagree with the idea that these teens were using chemicals to deal with life as opposed to developing life skills which are in essence the developmental work of adolescence. As a result, these teens come to us significantly impaired and highly immature. This very immaturity makes treatment difficult because the twelve-step model is a model that presupposes a certain level of mature functioning. Our goals must include assisting the adolescent in achieving some level of recovery as well as some level of maturity.

ASSUMPTION #6:
Addicted teens are
multi-problem teens.

In order to treat teens effectively, we must be prepared to provide comprehensive treatment which addresses whatever issues surface with the adolescents. The majority of teens who present for substance abuse treatment have a long history of problems which predate their use of chemicals (CATOR, 1987). Some of these problems carry with them a diagnosis such as depression or attention deficit hyperactive disorder. Some of these problems are just as significant but do not carry a specific diagnosis, such as sexual and physical abuse, addicted parents, poor self image, limited life skill development.

It is unrealistic to expect that treating these teens for substance abuse will eliminate the problems that these young people have been struggling with for years. However, unless the adolescent is able to remain free of chemicals, the other issues will not be resolved and the adolescent will not experience stabilization in regards to an accompanying diagnosis. While it is crucial to address the substance abuse as a primary disorder, other primary issues cannot be ignored if the goal is to assist the teen in improving his/her level of functioning.

CHAPTER
2

ADOLESCENT DEVELOPMENTAL ISSUES WHICH MAKE TREATMENT DIFFICULT

Adolescence is a critical developmental phase marked by critical developmental tasks. It is often difficult to realize that, although adolescents may look physically mature, they are growing and changing from a cognitive, social, and emotional perspective. These developmental tasks, combined with the dynamics of their addiction, make treatment of substance abuse and psychiatric disorders, as well as therapy in general, a difficult and challenging undertaking. Unfortunately, many treatment approaches continue to have adult expectations for adolescents. These expectations are developmentally inappropriate and are doomed to fail.

This chapter will look at eight specific developmental tasks which make treatment challenging for this population. It is important to keep in mind that these are developmental tasks faced by all adolescents, not just addicted adolescents. Treatment will be more successful when we recognize and respect the developmental implications for this population.

1. Cognitive Development. During early adolescence, the adolescent's ability to think in an abstract fashion begins to surface. It is important to keep in mind that the development of high-level conceptual thinking is a task with which adolescents struggle throughout their teenage years. It is a task that is not accomplished until young adulthood. As their cognitive abilities develop, adolescents begin to realize that, for the first time in their lives, they have the ability to think about and analyze what others are saying to them and make their own decisions regarding their opinion about what they are being told.

When attempting to master a new developmental task, children and adolescents often appear preoccupied with the task until it is something they can accomplish with ease. A significant part of developing abstract thinking skills includes the emergence of independence and critical thought. During early adolescence, teenagers are fascinated by their ability to think independently and critically. Most generally, they are thinking independently and critically about whatever they are being told by the adults in their lives. The process sounds a bit like this: "Who said? Why do we have to do it this way? Who made up this stuff? Why should I believe you just because you said this is the way it is?" As a result, adults tend to react to adolescents practicing the development of their independent critical thinking skills by labeling them as resistant. It is helpful to keep in mind that adolescents love to think about thinking. If adolescents can be cognitively intrigued by the material they are being presented and are allowed to develop their own twist to it, they are much more accepting.

It is important to keep in mind that we often present abstract concepts, particularly concepts borrowed from the twelve-step program, which are developmentally inappropriate and beyond the grasp of the adolescents with whom we are working. It is my experience that many adolescents would rather die than acknowledge that they did not understand what someone was saying to them. These adolescents play "smart" and look at us as if they understand because their image and fear of looking dumb prevents them from telling us that they don't have a clue as to what we are saying to them. When adolescents feel stupid, it is very likely that they will either act as though they understand what we are saying or will become angry and hostile. When we use concepts and questions that are beyond the grasp of the adolescents with whom we work, we are inviting hostility and resistance and setting up failure.

2. Language Skill Development. Development of language skills is often overlooked as part of the adolescent process. It is important to keep in mind that as adolescents begin to think about things in a different way, they must develop language skills which allow them to communicate what they are thinking. It is incorrect to assume that cognitive development and language skill development are always consistent. There is a time in early adolescence when the cognitive ability of some teenagers is more advanced than their language skills. As a result, adolescents often have a difficult time explaining what they are thinking or explaining their behavior. As long as treatment of adolescents gages their success by their ability to interact verbally, there will be a significant number of adolescents who will be left out of the process.

I enjoy watching the television show "Wonder Years" because I think it provides wonderful examples of adolescent development. A few years ago, there was an episode in which the main character, Kevin, entered ninth grade. He had an absolutely horrible first day of school. Throughout the course of the day he kept telling himself that he could not wait for the end of the day when he could connect with his girlfriend, Winnie, as she would be the one person who would understand. He planned to pour his heart out to her when he saw her. At the end of the day he saw Winnie, who asked him, "How was your day?" Kevin looked at Winnie, sighed and stated, "Fine". The voice in the back of Kevin's head said, "Sometimes when you're fourteen, life is difficult to put into words." All professionals who work with adolescents would do well to remember that sometimes it is difficult for adolescents to express verbally what is going on with them.

3. Developing Boundary Systems. Successful completion of adolescence requires that teenagers emerge from this phase having established some boundaries. These boundaries allow them to feel that they are individuals within their family system and within society. Most of us agree that it is important for adolescents to develop boundaries or they will grow up as nonfunctional and pathological adults. However, it is often difficult for us to accept that their boundaries extend to us. For example, adolescents establish boundaries within their families by deciding who their friends will be, what they will wear, what music they will choose, when they will be hugged and who they will hug. Perhaps even more painful for families, adolescents decide to build their own life. This life does not include their family in all that they do. As a result, they become preoccupied with privacy, secrets, and space.

It is important to teach adolescents appropriate methods for developing boundary systems. Adults who interact with adolescents often forget this and are disrespectful of teen boundaries. One boundary issue that surfaces in a helping relationship is that adolescents need time to decide whether or not they like the professional who is working with them and whether or not they feel the professional is a trustworthy individual. I strongly believe that we are often disrespectful of adolescents and expect them, in fact push them, to disclose information that we feel they need to talk about before they have had a chance to decide whether or not we are trustworthy individuals.

4. Action Versus Talk Orientation. Young adolescents, in particular, are more likely to use activity and action rather than talk to express their feelings. Anyone who has ever worked with a group of junior high adolescents knows that most of their interactions are marked by physical activity. They express their affection for one another and their bonding by patting one another on the head, punching each other in the arm, and slapping one another on the back. I know one young adolescent who reaches over and shakes my foot when he wants to make sure that I am listening to what he is saying.

Adolescents are very likely to use action to defend against conflict and resolve disagreements. This high level of activity is often exhausting to adults. Young adolescents work through their issues by moving their bodies. If an adolescent is reluctant to talk, I often suggest that once you get their bodies moving, their mouths will follow. They are also very prone to relieve anxiety or bond with their social group through horse play. Horseplay is rowdy and distracting and usually against the rules in most treatment environments. Not allowing horseplay with young adolescents is actually developmentally inappropriate. We also expect young adolescents to verbalize their feelings in a very adult way. Working with teenagers in a way that is respectful of them includes providing them with physical outlets as well as a variety of ways in which to express themselves other than talking.

5. Devaluing Adults. Adolescents view adults, even helping professionals, as being different than they are. This is part of establishing their own identity and fighting for their right to develop their own opinions and attitudes. Young adolescents (13 and 14-year-olds) tend, as a group, to like adults one-on-one, but are too embarrassed to admit this to their peers. Middle adolescents (15 and 16-year-olds) tend to do much better in groups because most 15 and 16-year-olds do not have relationships with adults other than their parents. Older adolescents (17 and 18-year-olds) are usually in the process of rejoining the adult population and actually like to engage in therapeutic relationships with adults. This means that adolescents may have a very difficult time developing relationships with older adult sponsors. I personally promote utilizing other recovering adolescents and young adults as sponsors for adolescents.

Due to this devaluing process, adolescents frequently question adults and challenge their opinions. It is important not to take it personally when adolescents question us. A question does not always imply resistance. It is often an appropriate behavior for an adolescent.

6. The Importance of the Peer. Adolescents establish their identity through their association with their peer group. Adolescents, particularly young adolescents and middle adolescents, are deathly afraid of being scapegoated or rejected. Young adolescents in particular, are very uncomfortable with the process of confronting one another. In fact, with young adolescents the most pathological member of the group gains the most status. Most young adolescents, chemically dependent or not, will not confront peer behavior even if the behavior goes against their value system. In developing treatment programs, it is important not to judge adolescents' success based on the extent to which they confront their peers. A great deal of reframing work needs to be done to teach adolescents how to confront appropriately and even to teach them that confrontation is help.

7. Personal Fable Thinking. Adults are often amazed at the adolescent's ability to maintain personal fables. Personal fables very simply are the adolescent's view that, "This won't happen to me," as they often say in my adolescent group—"I'm unique." All adolescents have their own personal fable. Some very common personal fables are: "I know that when other people have sex without using birth control they get pregnant, but that won't happen to me." "I know that when other people drink and drive, their driving is impaired, but not mine." It is important to remember that even healthy adolescents experience a frustrating level of personal fable thinking.

I repeatedly go through the following scenario when talking to teens who are in danger of not receiving any credits for the entire academic year because their grades are all F's. Each of these adolescents, usually sophomores, tells me not to worry, that they will be able to receive credit for their classes. When I point out to them that I do not understand how they will pass, since they are actually flunking all their courses, they usually point out to me that they have four weeks left in the school year and remind me that they are good in the crunch. Inevitably, at the end of the school year these adolescents come to my office devastated. They often report to me in a very surprised manner that they flunked all their classes, did not receive any credits for the year, and will not be able to advance their status. It always amazes me that they are totally surprised by this.

Personal fable thinking, coupled with the denial of addiction, often drives adults crazy. The only cure for personal fable thinking is that eventually adolescents have enough life experiences which contradict their fables that their thinking becomes more realistic. Adults can facilitate this by making predictions and pointing out facts. We should not be surprised when adolescents continue in their personal fable. Personal fable thinking does contribute to relapse and slips for addicted adolescents.

8. Lack of Living Skills. Adolescence is all about developing social skills, social competence, problem-solving skills, and impulse control. In working with adolescents, we often get angry that they have not perfected these skills as opposed to understanding that it will take them several years to develop these skills in order to be on a par with adults. One of my primary concerns about traditional treatment approaches is the practice of telling adolescents that the twelve-step program of recovery will keep them clean and sober; adolescents do not have the cognitive skills, social skills or problem-solving skills to access this program and make it work for them. An important part of treatment of all adolescents is to teach basic life skills for recovery and to teach them skills they need to access AA and NA. The concept is further explored in the author's first book, *Professional's Guide to Dual Disorders of Adolescents* (Gabe, 1989).

It is with this understanding of the unique developmental tasks of adolescents that the rest of the material in this book is laid forth. It is my hope that, as professionals, we become increasingly aware of the developmental implications when treating this unique population.

CHAPTER

3

UNDERSTANDING TEENS AND NEGATIVE SUBCULTURES

Few professionals will argue against the fact that traditional addiction treatment was designed for middle-aged, adult male alcoholics. When polydrug users became integrated into the traditional treatment environment, they presented challenges which the original treatment program designs were not prepared to address. Treatment of adolescents presents further challenges to this particular model. The recent recognition of the prevalence of coexisting psychiatric diagnosis among substance abusing adolescents complicates the treatment process even further.

It is important to understand the differences between traditional adult alcoholics and adolescent polydrug users.

Many traditional alcoholic adults and adult prescription drug users are mainstream culture individuals. While these individuals may be required periodically to venture outside their mainstream culture environments in order to maintain their addiction, they are not active members of a negative subculture.

In fact, these individuals are often valuable and contributing members of the mainstream culture. They are in essence, "belongers." They belong to extended families, community organizations, churches and clubs. Many of them have traditionally possessed a mainstream value orientation. This value orientation plays a significant part in the first step of the AA or NA program. The first step is powerful because when alcoholic individuals take a look at their use and realize they have strayed from their value system in order to maintain their use, they experience the pain which often motivates them to recover.

Many traditional treatment approaches with alcoholic and chemically dependent individuals are built around the fact that these individuals will experience guilt and remorse about their drug using behavior. This is often not the case when dealing with adolescent addicts. As adolescents begin using polydrugs, they quickly deviate from the mainstream culture into a drug using subculture in order to sustain their use. When adolescents are exposed to negative subcultures at an early age, they become socialized by these cultures. Polydrug using adolescents progressively lose touch with the mainstream culture and are heavily exposed to negative subcultures at the vulnerable ages of twelve, thirteen or fourteen. These are adolescents whose character development, attitudes, values, and morals are significantly influenced by the drug using cultures.

This early exposure lays the groundwork for addiction as well as characterlogical depression and conduct disorders. It is often difficult to motivate these young people to change because they have no regrets about their drug using behavior.

We are also noting a significant number of adolescents who are second and third generation polydrug addicted individuals. Treatment professionals often report seeing adolescents who are second generation gang members, polydrug users, and second generation satanic cult members. These adolescents have been born and raised in unhealthy and negative subcultures which make treatment and prevention even more difficult.

Cultures promote a group of norms which maintain, sustain, and reinforce a particular set of values, behaviors, and attitudes. Mainstream cultures socialize children by teaching them to adopt attitudes, values, and behaviors which will assist them to function in our society. Subcultures teach individuals an alternative set of values, attitudes, and behaviors which assist individuals in functioning effectively within the subcultures. Primary subcultures of today's youth include satanism, drugs, and gangs. Subcultures vary depending on geography. For example, I have from time to time worked with highly intelligent adolescents from a very affluent community who were members of an extremely sophisticated computer hacking criminal subculture. These youths were as strongly influenced by this subculture as are young gang members by their subculture.

Professionals and lay people are voicing a tremendous concern about the fact that adolescents are different today than they were five years ago. Some of the differences that are routinely cited include feelings that today's youth are more violent, lack mainstream culture goals, are more disrespectful of authority and society, more exploitive of others, more impulsive and careless, and have a weaker sense of what's right and wrong. Many professionals find themselves shaking their heads after young people leave their offices and asking themselves, "What makes these kids tick, and where did they come from?" I have been working with adolescents for thirteen years and I find these reactions to be consistent with my own observations.

When dealing with adolescents whose value development has been significantly influenced by negative subcultures, it is ineffective to approach these adolescents as though they have a mainstream value orientation. I firmly believe that in order to intervene effectively with many of the youth of today, it is critical to understand the significance of the subcultures in their socialization, their drug use, and their pathology. In order to understand this, it's important to understand what factors in our communities, in our families and in society contribute to the fact that our youth are so vulnerable to what the subcultures have to offer. When treating addicted and dually diagnosed teens, it is often difficult to engage them in the process of change or recovery without first disengaging them from their negative subcultures. Continued involvement in the subculture leads to relapse and sabotages any attempts at change. This chapter will examine the current phenomenon of adolescent subculture involvement. The next chapter will explore specific techniques designed to disengage adolescents from negative subcultures.

THE SOCIALIZATION OF KIDS IN AMERICA

In order to appreciate fully the role of subcultures in socializing the youth of today, it is important to examine how youths in our culture have traditionally been socialized. For many generations, children were born and raised in our society with very little thought given as to how kids are socialized. The average American family took for granted that if they did a good job parenting, kids would grow up and adopt mainstream value orientation. This happened for many generations in our society. However, our society has significantly changed in the last twenty years. Elements of our culture that have traditionally been in place and provided opportunities for socialization are no longer present. As a result, we are being introduced to a generation of youth who have not been socialized and families, communities, and professionals are wondering why.

As a society, perhaps we have taken for granted how kids have received socialization. The most obvious source of socialization is the family. Traditionally in American society, families have included parents as well as extended family (grandparents, aunts, uncles, and cousins). Parents have traditionally taken an active role in teaching, through words as well as actions, values and morals. When an extended family is actively involved in a child's life, they reinforce the values being promoted by the parents. As an adult, I often recall my grandmother's voice clearly instructing me on what was right and wrong.

In today's society, children spend less time with their parents as a result of an increase in single parent homes as well as an increase in the number of children who live in families where both parents work. In addition to this, we are now a mobile society where children often live a significant distance from any extended family. Grandparents and other extended family members have a difficult time assisting in socializing children when they see the children infrequently. Parents today have less assistance from their extended families in raising their children. This is a day and age when parents with less time than ever have less help than ever in raising their children. This is an issue of resources which impacts our entire society and it is an issue that needs to be taken seriously.

Neighborhoods have traditionally played an important role in the socialization process. I recall my own childhood growing up in neighborhoods where everyone knew everyone else and everyone watched out for one another. As an adolescent, I lived in a community where everyone left their keys in their car, in case the neighbors had an emergency and had to borrow the car. In addition, my brothers and sisters and I felt that we couldn't get away with anything because if our mother didn't see us, a neighbor did and would quickly report any misbehavior to our parents. We were given very clear messages about appropriate behavior and developed morals and values based on consistent accountability for our behavior.

I presently live in a neighborhood where I have resided for four years. In that time, all but one of the families on my street has moved. It's difficult to know one's neighbors in these circumstances. I recently strolled out to our street to chat with one of the children who was new in the neighborhood. As I approached her to introduce myself, her older sister yelled, "Stranger!Danger!" I quickly looked around to figure out who this stranger was on the street when I realized that they were talking about me. It's difficult to play a role in the socialization process when you do not know the families who live next door.

Institutions have traditionally played a significant role in the socialization process by further reinforcing the values promoted in family. Among these institutions, schools were very significant. Small schools which served neighborhoods promoted a sense of partnership between the families and the educational community. Parents often knew teachers and would see them on a regular basis and the schools were small enough that students could feel significant. In many communities today, children attend schools that are a considerable distance from their homes. Parents and teachers do not connect on a regular basis unless a great effort is made to do so by both the parents and the educator.

In many communities, students in the sixth grade become part of the huge middle school system where they often get lost.

Churches, youth organizations, and clubs contribute to the socialization process for kids. We have a difficult time maintaining organizations such as the Boy Scouts because these organizations rely heavily on volunteers. With the increasing demand on each individual's time, volunteers become more and more difficult to find. Schools, activities, sports and organizations provide kids with an opportunity to develop skills (problem solving skills, social skills, and organizational skills). They also help children develop a sense of competence and belonging. It is important to continue to make this resource available to children.

When discussing the issue of the socialization of today's youth, I often hear people blame the lack of socialization on children watching too much television, seeing too many violent movies, and listening to music that promotes subculture values. Television, movies and music would not be a threat to the socialization of our young people if they were balanced by a strong influence from family, extended family, neighborhood, and institutions. However, in the absence of the other factors, music, television, and movies do play an important role in how our children view the world and view themselves. The fact that our kids can be so easily influenced by the media is an indication that the traditional means of socialization of children has significantly deteriorated.

Historically, parents had a great deal of assistance in socializing their children. Parents sent consistent messages to children and the child's extended family, school, and neighborhood reinforced these messages. Today, at a time when parents have less time and less energy, they are faced with the awesome task of socializing their children and they face this task with less support than the generations of parents before them. In effect, parents are being asked to do more with less. At a time when parents need more support than ever in raising their families, they are receiving less.

WHY ADOLESCENTS CHOOSE SUBCULTURES

I often feel that we are in fierce competition with the subcultures for our youth. In order to understand this competition, it is important to examine what the subcultures offer that is so attractive to high-risk adolescents. In order to understand this, I began to explore the research on resiliency factors. Resiliency factors refer to protective factors for high-risk kids. When researching resiliency, people ask the question, "Why do some individuals who grow up in very high-risk environments have problems, while others are able to live in high-risk environments and continue to function without having problems?"

In reading the research, it strikes me that resiliency factors are very simply things that kids need to grow and develop. When our mainstream culture cannot provide these things for our youth, they will seek to get these needs met in an alternate fashion. These needs and alternate methods are as follows:

1. KIDS NEED A SENSE OF COMPETENCE.

Resilient kids are kids who feel some sense of competence in their environment. Resilient kids are kids who feel they have some influence and control over what happens in their environment and their life. They possess coping skills which help them in approaching and solving problems, controlling their impulses, interacting with others in a socially appropriate manner, feeling like worthwhile contributors and competent individuals. Competence equals power. When kids feel some sense of power, very important needs are being met.

**Negative subcultures provide
a place for high-risk kids
to feel competent.**

Children and adolescents who feel incompetent in their communities and in their families, will actively search for a place where they feel they fit. Children who have learning disabilities, attention deficit disorders, and a lack of social skills often seek refuge in subcultures. Kids with limited life skills, limited academic ability, and limited verbal skills can be contributing and functioning members of drug cultures, gangs and cults. Kids who feel stupid in the classroom and insignificant in their families can very easily feel important and smart in the subcultures. Subcultures promise kids power. The drug culture promises power through numbers and membership, gang cultures promise power through violence and intimidation, and satanic cultures promise power through evil. All subcultures promise power.

I discovered in my work with members of the computer hacker subculture, that this culture promised power through the information that could be illegally obtained by the computer hacking activities. When kids feel powerless in the mainstream culture, they will seek refuge and feel empowered in negative subcultures. High-risk kids are often kids who have been isolated from the mainstream culture since a very early age. They are often children whose inappropriate behavior in first grade becomes a legacy that follows them from year to year.

2. KIDS NEED A SENSE OF COMMITMENT TO CONVENTIONAL NORMS.

Research tells us that resilient kids are kids who have strong commitments to conventional (mainstream) norms and values. Resilient kids often describe themselves as achievement oriented, academically motivated, socially aware and socially concerned. Mainstream norms provide parameters which dictate appropriate social behaviors. Although children, and particularly adolescents, outwardly appear to rebel against parameters being set on their behavior, they desperately need these. Adolescents need to feel that adults, families, and institutions will step in to set limits on their behavior and provide them with guidance when they get out of control. Adolescence is a paradox of wanting to assert one's will but also hoping that someone will step in and protect one from oneself if one should get out of control. Norms provide adolescents and children with guidance, direction, and a sense of meaning and purpose.

Subcultures provide clearly
stated alternate norms.

Adolescents understand in no uncertain terms what behavior is expected and accepted in their subcultures. Gangs, cults, and drug cultures provide adolescents parameters within which they are expected to operate. Furthermore, members of these subcultures know very clearly what the consequences are for not adhering to the norms established by the culture. For example, adolescents who are members of gangs are able to articulate very clearly what the rules for gang behaviors are and what will happen if individuals deviate from these rules. The attraction of adolescents to these cultures speaks to the need that adolescents have for someone to establish clearly defined, clearly stated, and clearly reinforced norms for their behavior. Indeed, I know adolescents who are willing to risk their lives in order to obtain membership in a gang. Adolescents, as a result, are socialized by the norms of the subculture as opposed to the norms of the mainstream culture.

3. RESILIENT KIDS ARE INVOLVED WITH TRADITIONAL MAINSTREAM INSTITUTIONS.

Institutions such as churches, schools, social organizations extended family, and neighborhoods assist adolescents in developing coping skills, provide socialization to the mainstream value, and increase adolescents' sense of belonging and commitment to something larger than themselves. These institutions can be a source of support for adolescents and provide them a place to get needs met outside of the nuclear family system. The less the adolescent is involved in traditional institutions, the less opportunity they have to develop a sense of membership, increase their sense of competence, and experience a sense of commitment to the values taught and promoted by the institutions. Unfortunately, many of our high-risk kids become disengaged from institutions at an early age due to behavioral or learning problems.

I recently worked with a seven-year-old child with Attention Deficit Hyperactive Disorder. The child had a beautiful voice and loved to sing, but was not allowed to join the choir because the choir director noticed he was fidgety and felt he would be a distraction to the other children. This same child was labeled in school as a trouble maker. Consequently, at the age of seven, this child was already feeling incompetent and isolated from mainstream culture activities.

Subcultures are alternatives to traditional institutions for high-risk adolescents.

Subcultures provide environments that are adolescent friendly. They provide adolescents with places to go, people with whom to associate, and things to do. While providing this for kids, subcultures socialize kids in the same manner that traditional institutions have in the past. The more heavily the adolescent is involved in the subculture, the more their value and character development is influenced by the subculture.

Adolescents desperately need to feel they belong. Adolescents who feel they cannot fit in or do not fit in can easily find membership in a negative subculture group. Membership for adolescents focuses not only on inclusion, but exclusion. In order for membership to have any status, there needs to be a sense that not everyone can be a part of this organization or clique. While in reality, membership requirements for the negative subculture groups are fairly low (just about anybody can be a druggy), adolescents place a great value on this membership and act as if it were an exclusive club.

4. RESILIENT KIDS EXPERIENCE A SENSE OF AUTONOMY.

The word "autonomy" implies that adolescents are responsible, independent and contributing members of the mainstream culture. The less the kids are involved in the mainstream activity, the more limited their skills and competency in the mainstream culture. The less the kids are empowered to assume responsibility in a role of importance in the culture, the less autonomous they feel. Not many generations ago, our society was highly agricultural and rural. Adolescents were valuable, contributing members in the family business. During my own adolescence, I was the second oldest child in a family of seven and I was responsible for caring for my younger siblings. I often hated it at the time; however, I knew that my family needed me and depended on me. I not only felt like a valuable and contributing member of my family, I learned many valuable skills and developed confidence in my ability to take care of myself.

In addition, autonomy implies that adolescents are aware that they can impact the direction of their lives by the choices that they make. Resilient kids believe they can make decisions which will provide them with "a way out" of an unhealthy environment. In addition, these kids do not blame themselves for the problems experienced by the adults in their life.

Subcultures provide kids a sense of pseudo-autonomy.

Subcultures allow kids to pretend or feel as if they are being autonomous. Members of the subculture bond together around the themes of, "We don't care what 'they' say, we'll do our own thing." Kids mistake the rules of the subculture which promote a value that says, "We'll do whatever we want," as a feeling of autonomy. Kids often feel as if they are being autonomous because they feel that they are valuable, responsible, and contributing members in the subculture.

5. RESILIENT KIDS HAVE A SENSE OF SELF-ESTEEM AND SELF-WORTH.

The development of a sense of self-esteem and self-worth in an adolescent comes from having access to all the resiliency factors discussed and listed above. Developing self-esteem requires a cumulative experience of feeling valuable, capable, in control of oneself, and feeling safe from humiliation. Resilient kids know how to elicit positive feedback and affection from others. This assists them in feeling loving and capable (McIntyre, White, Youst, 1990).

> **If adolescents do not have a sense of self-esteem, they will settle for a self-image which they create with physical symbols and trappings of their subculture.**

Adolescents who do not feel confident in themselves often hide their fear and vulnerability behind a well-constructed image. Adolescents draw on the trappings of their subculture (hairstyle, clothes, jewelry, language, and slogans) and develop their self-image around their membership in the culture. External subculture trappings help adolescents hide from their feeling of rejection, fear, and vulnerability. Adolescents spend time developing an image that is consistent with their subculture as opposed to developing true self-esteem. Early in recovery, adolescents cling to the image for fear of exposing their real selves and opening themselves up for ridicule and rejection. Adolescents find a great deal of comfort and security with the images they project to the outside world.

FAMILY RESILIENCY FACTORS

Research suggests that there are protective factors operating in families which assist kids in being resilient.

> **Effective family management is a protective factor for high-risk kids.**

Effective family management includes a clearly defined hierarchy within the family structure, consistency and some predictability in family interactions, and the presence of family tradition and family rituals (Benard, 1991). As a therapist, I often feel that we are dealing with a generation of parents who are doubtful and uncertain about their parenting ability. Many parents do not want to raise their children in same manner in which they were raised because they feel their own parents were punitive and over-controlling. Parents who have not had effective parenting role-modeled to them often feel they do not have the skills they need to parent their own children. As a result, parental self-esteem is low. Parents are often hesitant and inconsistent in their attempts to provide leadership and direction in their families. Parents need support and permission to establish themselves as the heads of the household and the courage to proceed accordingly. Parents may often need the help of professionals and/or support groups in developing skills that will allow them to parent in a healthy manner and in a manner that is different from the way in which they were parented.

I recently had an adolescent in my office who was brought in by his parents because of a long list of problems, including shoplifting and marijuana use. It was obvious the young man did not want to talk to me, so I asked him to share his opinion about the whole situation. He asked me how much I was being paid to talk to him. He then informed me that he felt my fee was pretty cheap, considering that I was being paid to do his parents' dirty work. When I asked him what he meant, he informed me that his parents had not confronted him with his behavior or even discussed it with him. (I checked this out with his family and it was true.) He also informed me that his parents had no control over either him or his three adolescent and young adult brothers. His final statement about the whole affair was, "I wouldn't be here if my parents knew how to handle us kids. If you ask me, you've got the wrong person in your office." How does a professional respond to that?!

Another aspect of family management is the passing on of family rituals and family traditions. Adolescents and children love rituals and tradition. It helps establish family identity and predictability. Two years ago at Thanksgiving, I asked a group of adolescents what their families had planned for the holidays. Nine out of ten adolescents responded that their families really did not do anything special. When I asked parents about this, they indicated they did not plan anything because the teens just sat around and complained about having to spend a boring day with family members. How sad that these young people will not grow up with a strong sense of tradition to pass on to their children. How sad that they will miss out on the benefits of family holiday traditions. How sad that adults over react to adolescent complaints about family holidays being boring. Most adolescents I know complain that almost everything sounds boring, but once they participate, they admit that it was more fun than they thought it would be.

Subcultures demonstrate effective subculture management and adolescents find safety and comfort in this.

In the subcultures in which our adolescents are engaged, there is little doubt about who is in charge. The hierarchy may be informal or it may be very structured; nonetheless, it is clearly outlined. In addition, subcultures are rich with rituals and traditions which families often lack. In fact, an introduction into the subculture often takes place through an introduction to its rituals and symbols. Some believe that adolescents are attracted to satanism and/or gang membership through their curiosity about the subculture's rituals and symbols. It is not unusual to see very young children wearing gang colors, emulating gang members' clothing, and using gang signs. These children are not necessarily members of the subculture; however, adolescents and children are attracted to rituals and symbols and they are beginning their initiation into the subculture through this involvement.

A clearly stated, defined, and enforced family norm which does not tolerate or accept drug use is an important protective factor for high-risk kids.

Adolescents and children need family members to define, articulate, and enforce norms for family behavior. Enforcement of these norms plays an important role in socializing adolescents to the mainstream culture. Families need to feel confident that it is good and healthy for them to teach their children, "In this family, we do things in this manner." Although adolescents rebel against norms, it does not mean that they reject these norms. In fact, while they are appearing to rebel against many norms promoted by their parents, they are actually internalizing many of the family messages into their belief system.

Research indicates that resilient teens have family environments in which the adolescents clearly know what their families expect of them and clearly know what the consequences will be for inappropriate behavior. Furthermore, the adolescent's activities are monitored by parents and teens are held accountable for their actions. (Mercer, 1991)

A sense of family cohesion and emotional support are important resiliency factors.

Adolescents whose parents are not divorced at the onset of their puberty tend to be resilient as do adolescents who feel that they receive consistent emotional support. These are obviously key ingredients to an adolescent's feeling emotionally secure. Support has several dimensions and can be defined in the following way:

- Family members are physically and emotionally available as evidenced by parental involvement in the adolescent's school extracurricular activities.

- Families serve as a social and emotional resource for their teens (i.e. teens feel they can go their parents for advice and support).

- Parents and teens participate in frequent and in-depth conversations with one another(Mercer, 1991).

- Access to a family member who the adolescent views as wise and caring.

Subcultures provide peer group cohesion and peer emotional support.

It is not unusual for adolescents to seek membership and emotional support from their peers. Often however, when adolescents are members of negative subcultures, the peer group support within the culture takes the place of the role of the family for the adolescents. This increases the peer group's power in socializing the adolescent and decreases the family's power. Subculture influences tend to be stronger on adolescents who do not feel emotional support from their families and in families that lack cohesion.

Understanding the subculture influence on drug addicted and dually diagnosed adolescents is critical for all professionals who work with teens.

Initiating the process of recovery and the process of change for teens involves understanding the role the subcultures play in adolescent addiction as well as in their lives. Having developed an appreciation for and understanding of the role of subcultures in dealing with chemically dependent adolescents, it is now important to discuss techniques for disengaging adolescents from these negative subcultures.

CHAPTER

4

DISENGAGING ADOLESCENTS FROM UNHEALTHY CULTURES

Here we are just like a seed
To grow and nourish like a tree
A new beginning, a brand new day
To our higher power we will pray
There can be a better way
If we are clean just one more day.

(Recovery Prayer written by the Adolescent
Treatment Group at Fairbanks Hospital, 1992.)

A critical part of engaging adolescents in the recovery process is disengaging them from negative subcultures. We have traditionally approached chemically dependent and psychiatrically diagnosed adolescents by immediately attempting to reunite them with the mainstream culture. For adolescents who have the skills to function and compete in the mainstream culture, this is fine. However, it is important to remember that many addicted and dually diagnosed adolescents and young adults feel they are incompetent to function in the mainstream culture. This feeling of incompetence in the mainstream culture often plays a role in reactivating the adolescent's use of chemicals.

Disengaging adolescents from negative cultures is critical because continued involvement in the subculture will inevitably lead to the teen's relapse into chemical use and return to dysfunctional behavior. Techniques that are designed to engage kids in this process of change, while creating subcultures which promote recovery, are powerful treatment tools. Learning to create adolescent-friendly cultures of recovery is critical because the recovery subculture provides adolescents with an opportunity to learn the skills which will eventually help them to be competent members of the mainstream culture.

It is my belief that unhealthy subcultures and negative subcultures are highly successful in recruiting our youth because they know how to make their cultures attractive to adolescents. Treatment professionals often try to attract kids into recovery by offering a program that is more attractive to adults than to adolescents. Learning to develop adolescent-friendly cultures of change is the first step in making adolescent treatment specific to and attractive to the population which it serves.

I do not feel it is an overstatement to say that we are competing with negative subcultures for the lives and future of our youth. In my work with kids, I have coined a phrase, "It is important to fight a culture with a culture." In order to attract adolescents into the recovery process, and in order to reduce the rate of adolescent relapse, we must actively work to create in our communities, treatment centers, institutions, and schools cultures which promote change. These cultures must attract kids and meet their needs.

There are four basic guidelines that are important in attempting to establish healthy recovering cultures of change for adolescents:

1. THE CULTURES NEED TO BE FRIENDLY AND SPECIFIC TO THE POPULATION WHICH YOU ARE TRYING TO REACH.

In simple terms, the first step in establishing recovery subcultures for teens is to create environments which are adolescent-friendly. Adolescents in our community struggle with finding places to go where adolescents are welcome. We often hear complaints that the adolescents are taking over the shopping malls and bothering people in the places where they hang out. In the recovering community, we often hear complaints that adolescents are disruptive, silly, noisy, and messy. Adults in recovery often talk about the wonderful feelings of acceptance and belonging they experience when they attend self help meetings. Adolescents, on the other hand, often sense they do not fit in and are not welcome unless they are willing to "act" like little adults. Adolescents need places where they can be clean and sober and feel safe, welcome and accepted for who they are (i.e. teenagers).

We often decorate our offices and treatment environments to impress the wrong people. We usually create adult-oriented treatment environments that tolerate kids as opposed to welcoming them. These environments are often boring, sterile, intimidating, and foreign to adolescents. In consulting with many adolescent treatment programs around the country, one of the things that I frequently notice are walls that are painted white and are absolutely blank. When I ask why the walls are white, I am told that the walls are plain because when the kids are there, the staff wants them to focus on their recovery and on changing the problems that got them into treatment. I believe that white walls often symbolize what kids think of recovery. Their walls at home are often filled with symbols of the subcultures. These symbols are intense and exciting. It is hard to compete with an intense and exciting subculture with white walls.

Creating cultures that are adolescent friendly is a matter of respect. Using words that adolescents understand and material that is designed for them is an example of respect. For many years, we have attempted to use adult films and treatment literature that do not address adolescent issues. Similarly, we use words, phrases and concepts which the teens reject because they don't understand them.

The following scenario provides an example of what happens when we use inappropriate language with teens: An adolescent male walked into group therapy which was being led by a therapist and a social work student. He had cigarette burns on his arm from playing the game "chicken." The social work student grabbed his arm and exclaimed, "You've been self-mutilating!" The teen stood up, swore at the social worker and stormed out of the room. The counselor followed the teen and found him in a fit of rage, swearing about the social work student for accusing him of such activity. The youth exclaimed to the counselor, "I ain't doing that s _ _ _! I can't believe she said I was doing that s _ _ _ !!" After a brief pause, the kid looked up and asked the counselor, "What is that anyway?"

2. RECOVERY SUBCULTURES NEED TO BE EXCITING, VIBRANT, AND REWARDING.

Adults often view recovery in terms of serenity and peace. Many adolescents are not particularly interested in serenity, but they are interested in excitement and stimulation. In order to attract adolescents to recovery cultures, the culture needs to meet the adolescent's desire for excitement, fun and action.

3. WHEN INTRODUCING AN ADOLESCENT INTO CULTURES OF RECOVERY, WE NEED TO FOCUS ON WHAT THEY HAVE TO GAIN AND NOT EXCLUSIVELY ON WHAT THEY HAVE TO GIVE UP.

Very often over zealous adults launch into a tirade of listing for kids all the things they will have to give up if they want to pursue a recovering lifestyle. It is not unusual for adolescents to be entertaining the thought of engaging in a recovery process. These tentative adolescents are often frightened away by adults who inform them that if they want to achieve recovery, they must be willing to go to any lengths to do this. We then very quickly inform them that they will need to give up their friends, their music, their parties, their concerts, their dress, where they go, how they act, how they feel, etc. The end result is that we often frighten adolescents away before we ever have an opportunity to engage them. I often refer to adolescent counselors as "salesmen for change." It is difficult to sell the process of change when our focus is almost exclusively on the negatives associated with that change instead of the positives.

4. WHEN ATTEMPTING TO ENGAGE THE ADOLESCENT IN A RECOVERY CULTURE, IT IS IMPORTANT TO REMEMBER THAT YOU DO NOT TAKE THINGS FROM ADOLESCENTS UNLESS YOU GIVE THEM SOMETHING TO REPLACE WHAT YOU HAVE TAKEN.

Much of the resistance that we encounter with adolescents is due to the fact that we are very quick to strip them of symbols of their subculture while not offering them something to take the place of what they are losing. It does not surprise me that we encounter resistance. I often picture the resistance as adults attempting to yank away things that the adolescents value. The more the adults tug and nag, the tighter the adolescents hold onto things that are important to them. It is much easier to convince the adolescents to let go of symbols of their old drug culture with one hand if you can trade them replacement symbols of a recovering culture with the other hand.

Striving to create cultures of change is a concept and an attitude that requires professionals to view things from a different perspective. This perspective might challenge many of the views that professionals in treatment centers, psychiatric hospitals and behaviorally-oriented programs have traditionally held. Perhaps it is time for some of these views to be challenged.

The rest of this chapter is dedicated to offering specific and concrete examples of how to implement this concept in a variety of different settings with adolescents.

CREATING SYMBOLS AND RITUALS
FOR THE CULTURE OF CHANGE

Negative subcultures are full of symbols which appeal to young people and these symbols are adopted as badges of membership and belonging. Young people surround themselves with these symbols which are represented by the music they listen to, the posters on their walls, and their preoccupation with paraphernalia from gangs, drugs, and satanic cultures. The first level of involvement in any negative subculture begins with curiosity about its symbols. It is not unusual to see young children emulating the dress and hand signals used by older gang members. The children adopt these symbols because they are curious about them, they think they are cool, and it provides them with a method of identifying with older individuals whom they respect. This curiosity about the symbols serves as a recruitment for future generation gang members. Similarly, the first level of introduction to a satanic cult often happens through curiosity regarding that cult's symbols, such as the jewelry and the Satanic bible. These symbols serve as visual reminders and emotional anchors which can keep the adolescent locked into the negative subcultures.

Symbols and rituals have a strong appeal to adolescents. Due to the change in their cognitive development, adolescents are learning to think in an abstract fashion that allows them to view things symbolically and metaphorically. This new way of thinking intrigues teens and they enjoy practicing this skill at every available opportunity. Symbols are especially appealing because they provide teens with something concrete to look at, hold, or feel while they are thinking about things which are abstract.

Symbols also represent secrecy and exclusion of others. As far as adolescents are concerned, the best symbols are those that have some element of mystery (i.e., we know what this means, but if you are not one of us, you do not know).

The subcultures with which we are competing are rich with symbols. In order to compete with these subcultures, we must substitute symbols from the negative subcultures with symbols which represent recovery subcultures. It is important to keep in mind that young people often develop curiosity about the symbols of the negative subcultures before they develop an interest in gang membership or membership in a satanic cult. Therefore, one method of engaging adolescents in the process of change is to hook their curiosity about this process by providing symbols. With a little encouragement, the adolescents themselves can be very active participants in the development of these symbols. We currently have access to a limited number of symbols such as medallions, coins, and jewelry. In order to engage the adolescent's curiosity about symbols, we need to broaden our repertoire.

The following are examples adopted by several groups of adolescents with whom I have worked over the years. One particular group of adolescents was very interested in making friendship bracelets. They decided as a group to choose some neutral colors (i.e., colors that were not symbols for gangs) and make identical friendship bracelets for all the members of their treatment group. In the process of completing this project, they decided that group membership was important. They made several extra bracelets and wore these bracelets at all times. New group members would come into the group and immediately notice the bracelets and ask what they represented. Existing group members would inform them that in order to obtain a bracelet in that particular group, one would have to complete the first step and present it to the group. Interestingly enough, new group members who initially were not particularly interested in participation in the program would request the first step to complete so they could obtain a bracelet.

I once worked with a very industrious group of aftercare clients who decided that they wanted to earn some money for various recreational projects. They decided to sponsor a T-shirt contest and asked several young people in the recovering community to design a T-shirt with a recovery slogan. The requirement was that the slogans be original. Adolescents love secret codes and they picked slogans that were subtle in nature. Unless one was familiar with the program, he would not recognize the slogan.

As a therapist in that community, I purchased several of the T-shirts and kept a supply of them in my office. At certain points in the treatment process, I gave these shirts to specific teens. Eventually, every group member had a shirt and when new group members came in, they would request a shirt as well. It became a ritual that in order to obtain a recovery related T- shirt, they had to trade me a symbol of their addictive subculture. In the ritual of the exchange they handed me a piece of their old lifestyle, and in return I handed them a piece of their new lifestyle. This is an example of how you do not take things from adolescents without offering them something concrete to replace what you have taken. Symbols can take many forms and can consist of artwork, slogans, clothing, and jewelry that have particular meaning to the adolescents. These symbols provide them with anchors into the culture of change.

Rituals: The second level of involvement in a negative subculture involves learning the rituals of that subculture. Gangs, cults, and drug subcultures are filled with ritualistic behavior. Adolescents have a passion for rituals; they are intriguing and interesting and provide structure that is easy for adolescents to understand. Adolescents who are involved with gangs, satanic activity, organized criminal behavior and drug use have lives that are filled with ritualistic behavior. Without rituals, adolescents often feel bored, empty, and even lost.

It is important to create rituals of recovery which the adolescent can use to replace the rituals of use. In developing a relapse prevention plan, one needs to include recovery-related rituals to take the place of drug using rituals and other unhealthy life style behaviors. Treatment, counseling, and therapy itself can provide rituals that are attractive to adolescents. Developing rituals for opening groups, closing groups, welcoming new members to groups, and terminating from groups are examples of integrating rituals into the treatment or therapy process.

Adolescents have their own unique way of developing and introducing new rituals. During one particular session of a group I once worked with, one group member was having a difficult week. I had a pencil with the Serenity Prayer printed on it. I handed the pencil to the group member to provide him with a symbol of support until our next group session. When the time came to close the next group session, the group members looked at me and reminded me that we could not close group until the pencil was passed on to the individual who needed it the most.

This ritual went on for several group sessions, and the pencil was eventually passed on to a particularly forgetful and unorganized group member. When the time came for that member to pass the pencil on, he sheepishly looked at the group and confided in them that he had lost the pencil. The group members were beside themselves and quite upset that their ritual had been interrupted. They quickly looked at me to provide another pencil and I had to inform them that I had only one. After the session I found myself scurrying to find another of the pencils so the group could continue its ritual. I quickly learned that for adolescents, something you do one time may quickly turn into a ritual for them.

Membership: Membership is the key attraction to negative subcultures. A sense of belonging and acceptance, and a sense of being part of something bigger than oneself are important to adolescents. In order to attract adolescents to a culture of change and to keep them engaged in this culture, membership into this culture has to be perceived as special and important. Since membership in a treatment or recovery group is often the first level of involvement in the recovery culture, membership focus is important. Making the membership attractive to the adolescent is a very important part of the process.

Allowing the group to select a name for itself which represents the group values and norms is a nice way to start this process. When directing a group to select a name, it is important to ask them to keep it simple, to keep it short, and keep it positive. Once the group name is selected, the name needs to stand even though group members will come and go. This helps provide a sense of positive ongoing culture within the group and provides the adolescents with the sense of being part of some thing bigger than themselves. They take a great delight in knowing that many people have been through the group before them and that many people will be there after they leave.

Once the name is selected, provide the group with a scrap book and allow group members to record the date the group was formed and do an entry on the meaning of the name. A termination ritual for the group includes having group members who are ready to leave the group write a note of inspiration and hope for members who will join the group in the future. This is signed with first name or initials and dates only. When new members enter the group, part of their orientation ritual is to spend some time looking over the scrapbook. This review provides the adolescent with a sense that they are participating in something that is important. It also provides them with hope and inspiration and significantly reduces resistance to the process.

I often encourage groups to develop a group closing or a group prayer to close their group therapy sessions. I instruct them to develop something short and simple, usually no more than six lines. As time goes on and group members change, they are asked to develop new group prayers. The old prayer is printed up, dated and placed on the wall. It does not take long to have an entire group therapy room filled with group prayers developed and designed by group members who were there before them. This also helps adolescents to develop an understanding of how spirituality can work for them in the program. The recovery prayer at the beginning of this chapter is an example of such a group prayer. Similarly, when group members come up with wisdom-filled or catchy phrases, we write them down and put them on the group room wall. Group members use them when trying to offer help and advice to others. This also encourages the teens in developing a language of recovery to take the place of their street language.

Ownership: One of the most powerful pulls of negative subcultures is the young person's sense of ownership in those cultures. For adults, AA and NA hold that same attraction because the program was designed for and by adult alcoholics and addicts. However, adolescents often do not feel that same sense of ownership in the program. This happens because they are often overpowered by adults in the program. I have come to realize that I am not sure exactly why the twelve step recovery program works for adolescents. I do believe that it works, but I believe that it works in a different way than it does for adults. From my experience, it works best when there are large numbers of young people involved in the program and when they take significant ownership for their own meetings.

I once worked in a community that had absolutely no resources for recovering young people. Two very charismatic adolescents decided that it was time to change that. They actively networked with other young people in the program and they found that this young people's group quickly grew in numbers to exceed fifty and sixty. This group also took a very active role in social activities for young people. They had bowling leagues for recovering adolescents, basketball leagues, frequent parties and dances, and even went to the extreme of renting the local YMCA on a regular basis. For the most part, adults knew which meetings young people would be attending and they stayed away. I continually heard complaints and in fact, made complaints myself that they were too loud, too rowdy, joking, and just not taking the program seriously. However, over the course of two or three years, there were literally hundreds of young people in that community active in the program.

They continue to come back, they continue to be an inspiration to other young people struggling for recovery, and it worked for them. Inevitably, as the adolescents grew and matured, they would seek some participation in meetings where "old timers" hung out and would talk about the wisdom to be learned there. While some adolescents feel comfortable in adult meetings from the very beginning, the majority of adolescents need to feel some sense of ownership for the program. Often they need to feel that there is a place where young people can go where they are welcome and accepted.

Values: As we have already discussed, negative subcultures promote their own value orientation. As a result of the participation in these subcultures, many of our young people experience value deficits. Focusing on recovering values is critical. In order to make this manageable, I like to focus on four or five basic values that the adolescents must have in order to stay clean and sober. I then talk about and teach about these values.

The values that young people need really depends on where their value deficits are. Values that are often appropriate to focus on during early recovery are the following:

1. Don't do anything that makes you feel like a loser or you will end up using over it.

2. It's important to be honest with yourself and those you care about.

3. It's not okay to mess people over to get what you want.

4. That little voice inside of you that says, "Don't do that, that's not a good idea."—you need to learn to listen to that voice.

Summary: It's amazing that adolescents who are not particularly interested in giving up their drugs are curious about cultures of change. It is my belief that we can overcome a great deal of resistance by creating cultures that intrigue and attract our young people. Once they develop a curiosity about the symbols and rituals of this culture and have some investment in membership in this culture, they will be more willing to give up their drugs. If you are working with young people who are not invested in the process of change, having them work to develop some of these cultural pieces serves as a very valuable group building tool. Most importantly, in developing cultures of recovery, one thing must be kept in mind—adolescents are adolescents above and beyond all else. If we want to engage them in the process of change, we must meet them at their level and meet their needs by providing cultures of change.

CHAPTER

5

DIMENSIONS OF RELAPSE

The most practical way to prevent adolescent relapse is to have a comprehensive understanding of this fairly complex clinical phenomenon. There are many different dimensions to individuals' personalities, to their lives, and to their recovery. These dimensions interact and interplay with one another to contribute to the relapse dynamic. In attempting to understand these dimensions, it is helpful to understand that these dimensions are very similar to characteristics of suicide as identified by Schneidman (Schneidman, 1985). These dimensions are important because they help us understand what relapse is like for the person who is caught up in the process. Most importantly, they help us to understand what makes relapse appear as a viable alternative for the individual who is experiencing it. This chapter will be devoted to exploring the situational, affective and cognitive aspects of relapse.

SITUATIONAL ASPECT OF RELAPSE

We have long understood that relapse is often triggered by precipitating events. These precipitating events usually involve some type of stimulating environment from which the individual seeks relief through the use of a mood altering chemical.

It is important to recognize that the situational dimension of relapse interacts with other dimensions of relapse.

In working with relapse prevention, it is critical to identify which dimension is the strongest activating force behind the relapse process. This allows us to target our interventions accordingly. The two common relapse stimuli in the situational dimension include unendurable psychological pain and frustrated psychological need. If the situational dimension involves unendurable psychological pain, return to the use of mood altering chemicals provides a temporary escape for the individual. Individuals are innately driven to move from a place of pain to a place of comfort. Addicted individuals have a tremendous amount of practice in medicating their pain through the use of mood altering chemicals. The psychological pain in early recovery is often tremendous for adolescents. The experience of this pain combined with a lack of skills designed to deal effectively with pain makes this a powerful dynamic.

When this pain becomes intolerable and emotions become unbearable, adolescents are at extremely high risk to use chemicals. Each individual has his own pain threshold and it is important in working with adolescents to establish how much psychological pain they can tolerate and endure before being at high risk. Most psychological pain involves not only the environmental situation but the adolescent's view or perception of the situation. Therefore, the situational aspect of relapse overlaps with the cognitive aspects of relapse which will be discussed later in this chapter.

Interventions are obvious at this level—it is important to find out what is causing the pain for the adolescent. It is important to keep in mind that what the adolescent views as important, adults may view as trivial. It has often been said that no one experiences emotions as intensely and acutely as growing and developing adolescents. Often the adolescents share with us their emotional and psychological pain and, as adults, it is hard for us to understand the significance of this pain, given the events surrounding it. The next level of intervention is to assist the adolescent in lessening the pain. Professionals sometimes erroneously believe that, in order to prevent adolescent relapse, they must eliminate the adolescent's psychological pain. Most adolescents have some tolerance for some level of psychological pain. The pain does not have to be eliminated, but reduced enough so that it is more tolerable for the teen. The second significant stimuli is frustrated psychological need. It is important to realize that relapse appears logical to individuals who are involved in this dynamic. It often appears logical because these individuals have a constricted focus and because it is a reaction to a frustrated psychological need. Trying to meet psychological needs is a core motivation for all human beings. By examining relapse from this perspective, it helps us understand our client's motivation. This is a complex concept in working with adolescents because although driven to fulfill their psychological needs, they often do not have the insight or the vocabulary to understand or explain what is driving their behavior. Common psychological frustration experienced by adolescents in recovery include the need to feel competent, the need for acceptance, the need for support and love, and the need to feel that they are somehow important in contributing to their school, family, or social circle.

Treatment interventions here are fairly simple. If an adolescent appears to be at risk of relapse as a result of a frustrated psychological need, it is the therapist's job first to assist the adolescent in understanding what it is they want or what they think might help them feel better. This helps them identify their needs. The next part of this process is designed to help them address that need. Since addicted adolescents are often psychologically dependent on their drug to medicate their needs, they often do not have a great deal of practice of getting their needs met in an appropriate fashion. It is not unusual to have adolescents anguished about their unfulfilling relationships with their parents. Their need for a different type of relationship often goes unfulfilled because the adolescent does not know how to obtain what they need from their parents or from others. It is the counselor's job to help adolescents address their frustrated psychological needs by identifying the needs and developing a concrete action plan for the fulfillment of that need.

AFFECTIVE DIMENSION OF RELAPSE

Although there are many components and dimensions to the relapse dynamic, one important dimension is the affective component in the relapse process. Common affective characteristics include feelings of hopelessness and helplessness, feelings of incompetence, feelings of loneliness, and ambivalence about whether or not to remain clean and sober.

It is very normal for adolescents to experience a wide range of emotions and to experience these emotions intensely. The process of adolescence as a developmental stage of life is designed to teach adolescents to understand and respect their emotions and to learn to tolerate a wide range of emotions. Adolescents early in recovery do not have a great deal of practice in understanding, tolerating, and managing their emotions.

Dually diagnosed adolescents are often frightened, confused, and disturbed by their troubling emotions. Many addicted adolescents feel that one of the greatest benefits of their chemical use is that it allows them not to feel. Once the chemical use is discontinued, adolescents in recovery have to learn to deal with all the emotions which they have previously avoided. In addition, there are a wide range of emotions that are connected with drug using behavior and early recovery. Adolescents often become chemically free and begin to realize that they have lost a lot of valuable time and are developmentally behind many of their nonaddicted peers. This adds to their emotional discomfort and their sense of emotional isolation. In addition, adolescents must deal with the guilt, shame and confusion about many of the drug using behaviors with which they were involved when they were actively addicted.

The common emotion experienced by adolescents in recovery is a sense of tremendous loss. This loss is related to many things. Giving up the drug makes them feel like they are losing their best friend. In addition, they must give up their self image, life styles, and peer groups and prepare to enter a world that seems totally foreign to them. Adolescents also experience a loss of what their life was like prior to the onset of their addiction. In early recovery, adolescents often reflect upon the devastation they have experienced as a result of their use of mood altering chemicals. These losses often include grieving for their childhood, their value system, their sense of self-esteem, and the fact that their addiction has robbed them of so much of their youth. The result of these losses is a tremendous grief response. This grief response results in feelings of helplessness and hopelessness during which adolescents are acutely aware of their emotional discomfort and also feel that there is nothing they can do to feel better and that no one can help them. In addition, they often feel lonely, isolated and not connected to others.

This emotional discomfort often results in an internal ambivalence about whether or not they should continue in the recovery process. Adolescents begin to think that recovery is too painful and too difficult for them. They struggle with their ambivalence on a daily basis for many months in early recovery.

The emotional dimension of the relapse dynamic is particularly strong with an adolescent and the following interventions are helpful:

1. Address the feelings of hopelessness and helplessness by providing adolescents an opportunity to grieve the losses they have experienced. It is important to assist the adolescent in understanding that the resolution of grief often takes an entire twelve months. Adolescents cannot grieve alone. They need an opportunity to talk about the intensity of their emotions without being accused of having a "pity party." Talking about grief and sharing it with others is the best way to resolve it. The adolescents may need some structured help in letting go of their old life styles. Many programs do creative things with assisting adolescents in facilitating their grief.

One very powerful activity is to encourage the adolescent to write a good-bye letter to their old life style and their drug of choice. I have found that letter writing is most helpful for adolescents when it is given to them as a very structured assignment. I often ask adolescents to write a letter to their drug of choice as if it is the last conversation they plan to have with this old friend. I want them to have an opportunity to experience and explore their grief fully during this activity. I ask them to identify what they will experience, what they appreciate about their old friend and what they will miss. I also ask them to write about how angry they are at their friend for turning on them and causing them so much pain. I ask the adolescents to explain to their drug of choice why it is time to say good-bye and I instruct the adolescents to end the letter with a final farewell. It is important to remember that while this is a helpful activity, and an activity which does move adolescents toward grief resolution, teens will still need an opportunity and time to work through this process.

Another letter writing activity that can be utilized to help the adolescents to grieve what they have lost as a result of their drug use is to ask them to write a letter of forgiveness to themselves. This letter includes any anger they have at their drug using selves, any understanding they now have of why they became involved in drug use, and making amends and forgiving themselves.

2. Challenge the adolescents' sense of hopelessness and helplessness. Help the adolescents realize that they are not hopeless and helpless because they have had to make many difficult decisions in order to get where they are currently. Encourage them to realize that they do have the ability to influence their lives based on the choices they make on a daily basis. It may be helpful to the adolescent to point out to them options for dealing with their emotions that they may not be able to see.

3. Attempt to relieve the emotion of loneliness. At this point in the relapse dynamic, adolescents must be connected with others. It has been my experience that adolescents have more support than they realize and it is important to mobilize this support. It is often helpful to explore their environment to find people who are significant to and concerned about the adolescents. This may include relatives, immediate family, individuals in the program, significant adults such as teachers and counselors, youth ministers, and friends. It is important to involve significant others in this intervention. If I am extremely concerned about an adolescent's loneliness, I may ask the adolescent's permission to contact some of these significant others and ask them to attend a session in my office. During this session, we discuss the adolescent's loneliness and the immediate need for emotional support. On several occasions I have set up a concerned persons network and have asked individuals in that network to make a commitment to spend time with the adolescent over the next 24 hours or at least to make a phone connection. This results in immediate relief for the adolescent. In fact, just being able to list significant others appears to decrease their sense of isolation.

COGNITIVE DIMENSION OF RELAPSE

The cognitive dimension of relapse is strongly rooted in the adolescent's denial. This denial includes faulty logic that actually makes sense to the adolescent. The end result is that what is an illogical conclusion may appear very sensible to the adolescent involved in the relapse dynamic. The adolescent's faulty cognitive maneuvers, as well as his beliefs about his addiction, his use and the world in general, are a critical part of the relapse dynamic. There are several features of the cognitive dimension which facilitate and predispose relapse. These are very destructive kinds of reasoning because they are faulty, defy the rules of logic, and can result in destructive behavior for the adolescent. Several examples of this faulty cognitive reasoning have been discussed throughout this book.

Whenever examining adolescent addiction, it is impossible not to discuss in detail the faulty cognition of these adolescents since this is such a core aspect of the addiction itself. Relapse logic is characterized by deductive analysis. The cognitive fallacy starts with the desire to use. The individual experiences discomfort and begins to tell himself, "I am uncomfortable emotionally, physically, socially or psychologically. I would feel more comfortable in a mood altered state where I can find some freedom from this distress. Therefore, I will use mood altering chemicals to change the way I feel."

Once the individual has convinced himself of the desire to use, the cognitive fallacy continues. The next task in the denial process is to rationalize or make it okay to use. The adolescent comes up with a variety of rationalizations that may sound totally unreasonable to others but appear to make sense to him. (These are more thoroughly discussed in the chapter on relapse intervention). Much of the fallacy and faulty logic centers around promises the adolescent makes to himself about the use. It is not unusual for adolescents to convince themselves that they will use in a controlled fashion, that they will not let the use to get out of control, and that the use will not be a problem unless someone else finds out.

Adolescents also develop a fallacy about the significance of their use. Most adolescents do not return to the use of mood-altering chemicals by making a conscious decision to return to active addiction. Most of them tell themselves they will use but it won't be significant because it will be "just this time." They downplay the significance of the event. Once the cognitive dimension of relapse begins to absorb adolescents' thought processes, cognitive constriction sets in. The adolescents begin to put on mental and cognitive blinders and are only able to see limited options and begin to view the use of mood-altering chemicals as a magical solution. These adolescents have tunnel vision. As the preoccupation with the use becomes worse, they begin to make very poor decisions regarding their life and their behavior. They become extremely frustrated and irritable and they overact to emotional situations. Due to their cognitive constrictions, they are often not receptive to suggestions by others on how to improve things. They begin to ruminate about how bad the situation is and convince themselves that they have nothing to lose by returning to use because things could not possibly be any worse.

There are several interventions which are helpful in dealing with the cognitive aspect of relapse.

1. Explore the adolescent's logic. It is important to provide adolescents with an opportunity to talk about what they are thinking. The longer adolescents keep their thoughts to themselves and do not verbalize them, the more their cognitive fallacies appear to make sense to them. Adolescents usually appear surprised that others know that they are thinking about returning to the use of chemicals. This discussion can be initiated by inviting adolescents to talk about what has been going through their minds. Very simply make statements such as, "You know, I'm not sure about this but it wouldn't surprise me if you've been spending a lot of time thinking about getting high, particularly because there are so many things going on right now that are hard for you to deal with. For example, a lot of kids tell me that they often think that it would not be a problem to get high as long as no one else found out. Have you been thinking like that lately?" Adolescents always seem to be amazed by such simple intervention. They often look at me wide-eyed and say, "How did you know that?" Once adolescents begin to share with you their logic, two very important things happen: a. Once their faulty logic is verbalized, it does not make much sense to them and they begin to re-evaluate their beliefs. b. It provides an opportunity to challenge the logic in an attempt to modify it. This technique is discussed in further detail in the chapter that deals with relapse intervention.

2. Explore the fallacy about the significance of the event. When adolescents think about using mood-altering chemicals, they often think about the immediate relief they will feel but give very little thought to the long-term consequences. It is important to challenge this fallacy by walking them through the entire event. This can be done be acknowledging that being high will certainly feel good to them initially, and then encouraging them to explore the rest of the event. For example, ask them how they will feel when they go home to face their parents knowing that they have just used, how it will feel getting up the next morning, and how long they think it will be after the initial use before they have a very strong desire to repeat the incident. Adolescents do not think with a future-oriented perspective and guiding them to view the event in this way is helpful to them.

3. Broaden their tunnel vision. When adolescents become cognitively constricted, they begin to convince themselves that the only way they will feel better is to give in to their desire to use mood-altering chemicals. It is important to develop a list of other things that will certainly help them feel better. When developing this list, it is helpful to include things that are immediate and can provide immediate pleasure for the adolescent. These may include a listing of favorite songs, spending the evening with someone who is important to them, reviewing all their accomplishments in the last few weeks or months or rewarding themselves with a pleasurable activity. The adolescents may or may not choose to use the things on the list; however, making the list automatically broadens their tunnel vision and also reduces their anxiety.

4. Buy time. Since adolescents are impulsive and do not always appreciate that feelings are temporary, sometimes just buying time will assist the adolescent through the immediate crisis. I often do this by reminding adolescents that they always have the option to use. The old adage from the AA program which states, "You may always have another relapse but you may not always have another recovery," is very applicable here. Remind them that they always have the option to use, but they do not have to do that on this particular day. I have even asked adolescents to agree not to use just for the next twenty-four hours and that after that time period we would discuss it again. Amazingly enough, the vast majority of adolescents feel significantly better in a short period of time.

5. Surface the ambivalence. Even in a state of cognitive constriction, most adolescents who have had any time in a recovery program have ambivalence about throwing away all of their accomplishments to return to the use of mood-altering chemicals. It is important to search diligently to find any ambivalence that may exist within the adolescent and build on this ambivalence. In order to surface the ambivalence, I often ask adolescents, "Is there any little piece of you that knows that using right now would not be a good idea. And if so, what is that piece saying to you?" Just discussing these feelings and bringing them to the surface can be helpful to the adolescent. I may suggest that anytime within the next week when they feel like using, that they at least think about what they just told me and listen to that voice. Over the course of recovery, I try to teach people to tune in to and respect that voice. One adolescent I worked with identified the voice as "the thing that keeps me out of trouble."

6. Identify red flags. Once this cognitive constriction has been discussed, it is important to teach adolescents to recognize their cognitive dimension of relapse. This is very simply identified by the adolescent as their "druggy thinking." When the druggy thinking emerges, this is a danger sign that they need to slow down, not be suckered into this dishonesty, and share their thoughts with somebody.

These dimensions provide a comprehensive understanding of the relapse dynamic as it applies to adolescents. The next several chapters in this book are designed to build upon this understanding with a discussion of signs and symptoms of adolescent relapse, the process of managing relapse triggers and relapse intervention.

CHAPTER

6

THE DYNAMICS OF ADOLESCENT RELAPSE

Adolescent relapse has a dynamic that is unique to this special population. When working with addicted teens, it is important to understand the signs, symptoms, and progression of adolescent relapse. It is also important to provide teens with a framework for explaining the relapse dynamic that makes sense to them. Teens have a difficult time understanding the adult relapse material and, more importantly, teens do not believe that this information accurately describes their experience.

Many of the phases of relapse discussed in this chapter describe issues which teens will face in recovery and will eventually need to resolve if they are to have any hope of remaining free of chemicals. Borrowing from the adult model, the adolescent relapse model describes signs and symptoms which define a progression of the relapse state. In this model, relapse is outlined as following four distinct phases. These phases are described below.

PHASE I: ADJUSTMENT DIFFICULTY

Teens begin to struggle with phase one relapse issues very early in the recovery process. These issues include:

1. Feeling Uncomfortable with a Drug-Free Image. Almost as soon as teens enter into recovery and realize the need to develop a new self-image, they experience an identity crisis. Many drug-addicted teens have worked hard to develop an image consistent with their addiction and the subculture that sustains this addiction. They have placed all their energy and creativity into the druggy image which provides many payoffs to vulnerable adolescents. The external image provides emotional protection from the outside world. It is an image that says, "I don't care what you think," "You can't hurt me because I am tough," "I do not care if you accept me because me and my pals think you are stupid."

As many adolescents have explained to me over the years, the druggy image often provides protection from the greatest adolescent fear of all—being rejected by peer groups. This is clearly described by an adolescent who recently confided in me, "You know why we all became drug addicts, don't you, Janice? It's because we were all afraid of becoming nerds. When you have a choice of being labeled a burn-out or a nerd, a burn-out is always better."

The dilemma for the newly recovering teen is: If I am not a druggy, then who am I? Will I fit in anywhere else? Will I be able to find acceptance and make friends? How do I go about doing this? Can I face the world without my image? What will happen if I do?

Teens struggle with the following feelings and thoughts:

■ Don't know who they are if they are not a druggy.

■ Fail to develop a "fit" with a new peer group.

■ Start thinking about hanging around with old friends.

2. Lack of Confidence in Ability to Do Things Successfully. Early in recovery, teens become confused and overwhelmed by the task that faces them. They do not have a track record for making good decisions and they have not developed adequate skills to help them in making solid decisions. Teens respond to this lack of confidence in the following ways:

■ Try to develop a plan for solving all their problems at once.

■ Second guess themselves as they become concerned about making good decisions.

■ Feel overwhelmed and feel they cannot make all the changes required of them.

- Become afraid of and uncomfortable with feelings.
- Become preoccupied with problems at home and at school.
- Begin commenting that "this recovery stuff is lame and stupid."

3. Failure to Develop Appropriate Social Supports. Teens become painfully aware of their poor social skills at this stage. These are teens who while under the influence have very few fears. They have histories of high-risk behavior with little regard for their personal safety. However, in recovery, these teens are intimidated by simple adolescent tasks such as dancing or going to a party without being stoned. While they complain of being bored and lonely, they are reluctant to take the risks which are necessary to develop new friends or interests. They are painfully aware of their social awkwardness and begin longing for the sanctuary of the treatment center where companionship, structure and nurturing were provided for them with very little effort on their part. If one cannot have fun in recovery, recovery begins to become a burden and memories of the drug-using lifestyle become more and more attractive. At this point, teens are often:

- Feeling bored.
- Feeling lonely and isolated.
- Reluctant to take risks and leery about spontaneous and fun activities.
- Feeling uncomfortable in social situations without the use of drugs.
- Beginning to dwell on the treatment experience.
- Beginning to romanticize about the drug-using lifestyle.

4. Adolescents Do Not Feel Any Rewards For Living Chemically Free. When recovery becomes difficult, as it always does, teens become discouraged. Professionals, sponsors and parents sometimes unwittingly contribute to this by continually focusing on what the teen has to give up in order to stay with the program. We demand (sometimes prematurely) that they give up all their friends, their music, their hangouts, their clothes, the posters on their walls, their hairstyles, their earrings, their T-shirts, the way they think, act and feel, etc. By continually focusing on what teens have to give up as opposed to what they have to gain, we unwittingly talk kids out of recovery before they are ever really sold on the concept. Similarly, we take things away without giving them anything to replace what has been taken. Pat answers such as, "Well, recovery is lonely; if you want it badly enough you will just put up with it," do little to help the adolescent through this difficult phase.

Adolescents find that very early in the recovery process they are faced with emotional conflicts and uncomfortable feelings. It is not unusual for them to react negatively to what they are experiencing, particularly to problems they are having within their family. Many addicted teens do not have a framework for what healthy family conflict is. They often think that recovery will return their family to "the way it used to be." Many of the teens began using during their preadolescence, a time when family harmony is high and parents have not fallen off the pedestal in the teen's eyes. For addicted teens and their families to expect a return to this state is unrealistic. A healthy adolescent recently said to me, "Sure I fight with my parents; all teenagers fight with their parents once in a while. It's no big deal."

Recovering teens and their parents, on the other hand, often become discouraged when there is conflict in the home. They often interpret this as meaning that there is something wrong with their program.

In order to avoid dealing with difficult feelings on a daily basis, these teens might focus on the past (when I was using) or the future (when I can get out of the house). By doing this, they are not resolving issues and not putting into practice the coping skills that need to be fine-tuned in early recovery. Teens in this stage face the following:

- Begin to get in touch with issues their drugs have allowed them to avoid.
- View recovery only in terms of all they have to give up.

- Get stuck in thinking about the past or future and try to avoid the present.

- Become disenchanted with their family life.

- Feel angry about their addiction and the need for recovery.

5. Unable to Acknowledge Ambivalence or Conflicts. When adolescents struggle in recovery and talk about this struggle, they are working at staying clean. When adolescents become so afraid of the struggles they are experiencing that they avoid facing these struggles, they are in danger of relapsing. The stronger the need to avoid the ambivalence and the problems, the more dogmatic the adolescent becomes. This dogma is the teens' way of ignoring their vulnerability. It is typical at this phase to hear teens talk about seeing old friends. Instead of sharing that they feel lonely, isolated or sad that they can no longer associate with these friends, teens who are stuck will make comments such as, "It made me feel good to see them and realize what losers they are." "It did not bother me at all when I saw them; I just thought about how stupid they act when they are stoned."

One adolescent I worked with took this to a dangerous extreme. He agreed to cooperate with local law enforcement officers to set up buys to help bust the local drug dealers. He remained engaged in the culture of addiction and justified this by taking on a very self-righteous attitude. He continually spoke about the members of the local drug culture as if they were the slime of the earth. The more he focused on this, the more removed he became from a recovery program. This involvement, very predictably, lead to an eventual relapse.

Adolescents who sense they are close to using and who are frightened by the thought of using, are particularly dogmatic and overly confrontive with others who slip or talk about urges to use. It is easy for the professional to mistake this dogma for a strong commitment to recovery. I once had an adolescent call me and demand that he be allowed to transfer to my aftercare group. He indicated that he was tired of everyone in his group because they had all slipped and all the group focused on was relapse. He complained that he was determined never to use again and felt that the group was a waste of time for him. He stated that he wanted to be in a group that was serious about recovery. It soon became apparent that the young man was very close to using and was afraid of this possibility. A possible relapse would carry severe consequences. In order to avoid dealing with his fear, he denied having any trouble in recovery and was intolerant of others who expressed their problems. The young man relapsed within a month of the phone call, largely due to the fact that he refused to discuss his desire to use.

Symptoms of this phase include:

■ "I'll never use again" attitude.

■ "I can do this my way" attitude.

■ Becomes critical of and hostile toward users.

■ Intolerant of relapses and slips by others.

■ Not acknowledging or talking about urges, problems, or feelings.

■ Loses touch with sponsor.

PHASE II: EMOTIONAL AND BEHAVIORAL CRISES

If the adolescent is unable to resolve the issues in Phase I, the relapse dynamic becomes more problematic. Phase II begins. It is almost inevitable that most teens in recovery will face Phase II relapse issues at some point in their recovery.

6. Failure to Thrive. If adolescents feel they are not able to thrive in recovery, they become discouraged. Failure to thrive stems from living problems that all teens must resolve as they grow and mature.

When adolescents feel discouraged and overwhelmed, they find it easy to make poor decisions which result in irresponsible behavior.

Teens in this phase of relapse are struggling with developing balance and structure in their life. Balance and structure are an integral part of recovery, but are resisted by teens who have lived completely unstructured lives in their addiction.

While actively using, many of these teens stayed out all night, completely ignored the rules at home, and did not concern themselves with making responsible decisions at school. It is easy for teens to slip back into these behaviors, even in the absence of chemical use.

Teens may throw themselves into their recovery to the exclusion of all else, much as they threw themselves into their drug use. It is not unusual to see teens fluctuate from compulsive involvement in the program to almost no involvement.

For example, some teens try to go to school full time, work twenty-five hours a week, go to one or more meetings a day, stay out all night with other recovering teens, and try to do volunteer work. Other teens may lose structure in their lives and want to stay at home and sleep all day instead of going to school or meetings. Either of these extreme behaviors will create problems for the young person at home and at school. Teens begin to feel incompetent, but do not recognize how their behavior is creating problems. Teens in this phase struggle with the following:

- Loss of structure and balance in life.
- Adolescent oversleeps or undersleeps.
- Adolescent overworks or underworks.
- Adolescent isolates self or totally immerses self in peer group activity.
- Recovery plans are falling apart.
- Conflicts with family intensify.
- Return to old behaviors at school (tardiness, skipping).
- Blowing off responsibilities at home or on the job.
- Self-esteem is suffering.
- Adolescents feel they are going nowhere.

7. Anger. As teens struggle in recovery, they begin to get angry that things are so difficult for them. They often feel inadequate to deal with the many issues facing them in recovery and they struggle to develop skills that others their age have mastered comfortably. They feel they do not fit in. They become angry because they know that drug use will not help them find the answers they are looking for. As a result of this anger, they become resentful of the recovery program. Teens complain about going to meetings and hearing the same thing over and over again. Teens, who in their using days tolerated and accepted a great deal of abuse from their using friends, begin to develop unrealistically high expectations of their sponsors, counselors, and other friends in the program. They become critical of the same individuals who have given them rides to meetings, talked to them for hours on the phone, and supported them in recovery. They become particularly resentful of others who appear to be having an easier time in recovery than they are. The adolescent begins to associate with other teens who are struggling in the program and they reinforce one another's unhealthy behavior.

Symptoms of this stage include:

- Teens become more and more unhappy and become angry about their addiction.
- Teens begin building resentments.
- Teens begin to blame others for their problems.
- Teens become critical of the AA/NA Program.
- Teens become critical of strong program members.
- Teens begin associating with unhealthy program members.

8. Emotional Crisis. The emotional crisis is a culmination of all the relapse issues which have been identified thus far. All teens will face an emotional crisis at some point in the recovery process. This is the point in recovery when adolescents are faced with the realities of recovery and all the issues that their drug use helped them to avoid. This is the "make it or break" phase of recovery for teens. They will struggle with a great deal of emotional pain and will be faced with difficult decisions regarding what they will do at this phase. Many teens will experience slips, if they have not yet experienced them.

Family members, teachers and friends often think these adolescents are using at this phase because their behavior appears to be erratic and unreasonable. Families as well as professionals often demand that someone intervene in the teen's behavior. Teens frequently become so frightened that they will look for someone to rescue them. It is not unusual for teens to lie and make false confessions of using in order to be placed back into treatment in an attempt to avoid this painful and difficult period.

The only resolution to the emotional crisis is through it. If the process is interrupted by allowing the teens to escape back into treatment, the issues will resurface again in the future. This is a particularly trying time for professionals who work with teens as the teens often begin to feel frustrated, depressed, and overwhelmed. They make poor decisions which create problems for them, but they are unable to see this pattern of behavior. In fact, teens often try to solve problems by doing things which create more problems for them.

This pattern of behavior is clearly evident in the following example:

A fourteen year old male had been in recovery for four months and was actively involved in the recovery program. He attended meetings regularly, obtained a sponsor, attended weekly aftercare and also participated in individual counseling twice a month. The adolescent had been having problems with his family because he refused to obey the curfew at home. This adolescent had lived without any rules for the two years prior to treatment because his parents felt he was out of their control. The young man socialized a great deal in the program. He attended one or more meetings a night and after the meetings would spend hours in restaurants drinking coffee and visiting with other recovering teens. He attended all the social activities and would spend the night with friends from the program whether he had his parents' permission or not.

The young man did attend school, but frequently did not go to certain classes, or was often tardy. He made poor choices regarding his school work and had not made a lot of progress rebuilding his relationship with his teachers.

His poor choices were creating crisis for him in all areas of his life. He was frustrated and confused. He also experienced cognitive constriction. He appeared to be wearing blinders and could not make the connection between the problems he was experiencing and the decisions he was making. He was caught in an emotional tailspin that was very frustrating for the adults attempting to help him.

The young man was resistant to interventions attempted by his counselor and would often use his "program wisdom" to avoid taking responsibility for his decisions. When asked if he planned to attend school the next day, he would respond, "One day at a time; I don't know what I'll do tomorrow." When asked if he planned to go directly home after the AA meeting as his parents requested, he would respond, "First things first. First thing is the meeting. I don't know what I'll do after that." When confronted about his self-centered behavior he would respond, "It's a selfish program. At least I didn't drink or use today."

One particularly stormy day, the adolescent called in a state of crisis. He indicated he did not know where he was and stated he was calling from a pay phone. He said he had been in school and experienced a strong urge to get high. When he looked down the hall and caught sight of some old drug using friends, he panicked and ran from the building. He ran until he reached the pay phone and stopped. He came in for a session and reported that he was "sick and tired of being sick and tired." He maintained that he felt there was nothing wrong with his choice to run out of school in the middle of the day. The counselor pointed out that he started with one problem—the urge to use. His solution created several other problems, including unexcused absences from his afternoon classes as well as irate parents who were fed up with his poor school attendance. The counselor voiced concern that this young man was headed for a slip.

The following Monday, the young man called and reported that he had used over the weekend. His use was so severe that it frightened him and he asked to be readmitted to the hospital. He was told by his counselor that recovery takes place in the real world, not in the hospital. He was also told that he would have to deal with his decisions, behaviors and emotional crisis sooner or later, and that readmission would just postpone his coming to terms with his recovery.

He called another treatment center that did admit him and convinced him and his family that he needed long-term care. The young man was in the hospital for two days when he realized that he did not need to be there. He intentionally broke the rules so he would be kicked out. He left the unit with the treatment staff telling him that he did not have a shot at staying clean. The young man went back to his outpatient counselor, very willing to work to resolve his issues. He has been clean for many years and graduated from high school with honors.

This example demonstrates very clearly what happens at this phase in the relapse process. Adolescents will either return to use or will face and resolve their core recovery issues.

At this stage the following symptoms occur:

- Adolescent becomes locked into crisis behaviors.
- Adolescent loses the ability to problem solve or see healthy alternatives to current behavior.
- The adolescent's core issues surface and all seem to be coming to a head.
- The adolescent feels panicky.
- Impulsive behavior.
- Frustrated and irritable.
- Overreacts to stress.
- Feelings of depression and confusion.
- Adolescent becomes increasingly preoccupied with getting high.
- Adolescent's behavior creates a problem at home and school.
- Adolescent misuses the program to rationalize behavior and avoid taking responsibility to change.

If adolescents do not successfully negotiate this phase of recovery, they move into Phase III.

PHASE III: SETTING UP THE RELAPSE.

During this phase, adolescents engineer their own failure. They set the stage for relapse to occur.

9. Setting Up the Relapse. These adolescents are typically dishonest with themselves and others about their behavior and attitudes. They are making sure the drugs are available to them while trying to convince others that they are committed to recovery. It is not unusual for the teens to experience slips at this phase. The adolescents are attempting to prove to themselves that they are not addicted. This makes it easy for them to relapse without feeling bad about it.

Teens set up the relapse in the following ways:

- Exposing themselves to drugs and alcohol.
- Going to parties and not using.
- Going to parties and pretending to use.
- Making statements such as:
  — "I was just testing myself."
  — "I wanted to see if I could be around it and say 'no'."
  — "It did not bother me to be around it."
  — "I can still hang around with my old friends."
  — "I don't have to change my lifestyle."
- Calling old using friends.
- Hanging around at using places during school and free time.

10. Lose Respect for Their Disease. At this point adolescents avoid people who will confront them with the reality of their behavior. They may lie to themselves and tell themselves that they want to continue to be abstinent. They convince themselves and try to convince others that they will be able to do this without going to meetings or aftercare. The adolescent's motive at this point is to use and they are usually very dishonest about this motive. The adolescents lapse back into drug addicted thinking and spend a great deal of time convincing themselves that they will be able to use without experiencing any problems. They are usually able to convince themselves that using is not really the problem—the risk of getting caught is really the problem. Adolescents will demonstrate this loss of respect for their disease in the following ways:

- Cut down on meetings.
- Cut ties with recovering peers.
- Rationalize to make it okay to use.

PHASE IV: ACTIVE RELAPSE

The adolescent now moves into an active phase of relapse.

11. The Adolescent Using Chemicals Will Do One of Three Things:

- Tell someone about the use and try to get back on track with recovery.
- Tell someone and struggle with their ambivalence about whether or not they want to get back on track.
- Not tell anyone about the use and slip quickly into a complete relapse.

In order to determine the best way to intervene, one must know what the adolescent is thinking. It is important that the professional encourage adolescents to discuss the use and discuss their attitude about the use. For some teens, incidents of use frighten them and serve as a motivation to work harder at recovery. For other teens, a single incident of use confirms for them that they do not really want to work toward recovery. For teens who make a decision to continue their use, the relapse continues to progress.

12. Attempting to Control the Use. Adolescents at this phase of the relapse process have sincere intentions of controlling their use of mood-altering chemicals. They return to use with the idea that this time it will be different—this time they will control it. It is important to recognize that adolescents do have a period of time in the relapse process when they are successful at controlling their use. When they use once and experience no negative consequences or when they successfully control the amount they use, they are often totally convinced that this time will be different.

During this period of time, which may be a few days or a few months, adolescent denial is impenetrable. One cannot convince adolescents who are using in a controlled manner that they need to give up their use. In the past, kids would be rehospitalized if they used three times. These teens would sit in treatment sincerely believing that they had control over their use; treatment became a waste of time and money. Teens at this phase are best counseled from a relapse intervention mode (discussed in Chapter Ten). Adolescents are not usually ready to consider re-committing themselves to recovery until the final phases of the relapse process.

During this stage of attempting to control the use teens will:

- Use drug other than drug of choice.
- Attempt to set limits on use.
- Think they have control because they used once and nothing bad happened.
- Make self-conning statements such as:
  — "I just wanted to see if it would give me a better buzz since I've been off it for so long."
  — "I just wanted to see if I could use a little and hold it at that."
  — "I needed some money and thought I could deal but I don't plan to use it."
- Make excuses for use:
  — "I was getting fat and just needed to lose some weight."
  — "I just like the taste of beer."
  — "If it gets bad, I'll quit again."
  — "I'm not addicted; after all, I quit for (three months, six months, etc.)"

— "Things are so rotten, I might as well use."

— "My parents were bugging me and things were not getting any better."

■ Drop out of AA/NA.

■ Drop out of aftercare.

■ Lose touch with recovering friends.

■ Return to denial; unable to see the reality of the use.

13. Total Relapse. Teens at this stage will:

■ Return to heavy use.

■ Return to dysfunction as a result of the use.

■ Return to old peer group and old lifestyle.

14. Feeling Hopeless. Adolescents who have moved into the final phase of their relapse are adolescents who have lost control and recognize they have lost control. Adolescents who have been through this will tell you that they looked in the mirror one morning and realized that they had "blown it again." They are filled with shame and anger at themselves. They feel they cannot find their way back and are too embarrassed and humiliated to ask others for help. As the crisis around their use intensifies, these teens become more hopeless and depressed.

At this point adolescents will:

■ Recognize loss of control.

■ Develop a self-defeated attitude.

■ Feel they are lost and cannot find their way back.

■ Feel they have lost it all.

■ Feel that people who have helped them in the past are angry at them and do not want to be bothered by them.

■ Develop self-contempt.

■ Feel shame.

■ Develop suicidal ideations.

This is the time when adolescents are usually ready to accept help. Developing strategies for helping these teens at various phases of the relapse process will be discussed in great detail in subsequent chapters.

CHAPTER
7

ADDRESSING THE SLIP

We have established that many adolescents will experience slips (i.e., isolated incidents of use of mood-altering chemicals) while struggling to stabilize themselves in recovery. Professionals must recognize that this is a reality and be prepared to address these slips without giving teens the message that slips are expected and acceptable. Adolescents must know that the expectation in recovery is abstinence.

If adolescents have difficulty in achieving abstinence, our job as professionals is to focus on this. I frequently tell adolescents that the goal is for them to remain chemically free and I believe they can accomplish this; however, if they slip, my expectation is that they let me know. I try to impress upon them that slipping can be a detour or a dead end street. How they decide to handle a slip will determine what will happen in their recovery.

The goal is to focus the teens' behaviors, attitudes, thoughts and feelings back on the recovery track and help them to learn from their slip in order to reduce the chances of a future slip. In order to accomplish this, adolescents must understand and take responsibly for the behaviors, thoughts, situations, and emotional states which contributed to the return to use. The following questions were designed to address the slip in such a manner that adolescents learn from the experience.

These questions are:

- Where did you go?
- Who did you see?
- What were you looking for?
- What was going on with you in school, with friends, at home, with your feelings?
- What did you tell yourself to make it okay to use?
- What, if anything, is missing from your recovery program?
- How do you feel now?
- What do you want to do now?/What do you need to do differently?

The remainder of this chapter explores these questions in detail.

The first three questions are specifically designed to encourage adolescents to take responsibility for the behavior which precipitated the slip. When asking adolescents to explain the events that led up to the use of the alcohol or drug, professionals frequently meet with responses such as, "I don't know what happened. I was just driving around and the next thing I knew, I found myself in my dealer's driveway." If adolescents are to prevent future slips, they must be held accountable for decisions they made which resulted in a return to drug or alcohol use and comments such as the one above are not acceptable. They must answer the following questions:

- **Where did you go?**
- **Who did you see?**
- **What were you looking for?**

Although adolescents do sometimes unexpectedly find them selves in situations where drugs are available, most adolescents are in such situations because they made conscious or unconscious choices that placed them in these situations. Because of their delusional system, addicted adolescents may not be aware of how their choices directly or indirectly made them vulnerable to slips. For example, teens may report that they went to a birthday party for an old friend and did not realize that others would be drinking or using at the party, even when their history with these individuals would indicate that drugs would be available. Adolescents may say they went cruising with friends even though they knew the friends would be using, because they thought they could be there and not be tempted to use. These adolescents may sincerely believe what they are telling you. They may not recognize that their delusional thinking is precipitated by a desire to use.

This desire to use leads them to place themselves in situations where the drugs are available to them and slips are almost inevitable. We must teach adolescents to examine their choices and to acknowledge that when they make a decision to return to using places, see using friends, or look for drug-related excitement, these decisions are driven by a desire to use mood-altering chemicals. The only way to interrupt this process is to acknowledge this desire and be honest with one's self.

The next question is designed to assist the adolescent in identifying the social or emotional stressors which precipitated the use. Adolescents are much more likely than adults to slip as a result of their impulsiveness; therefore, not all their slips are precipitated by stress. However, if stressors are present, they need to be identified and resolved to prevent teens from slipping again because of the same issues. **We ask adolescents to take a look at what has been going on with their family, friends, school, and emotions.** It is not unusual to find that teens have returned to use following a painful or stressful event such as a fight with a parent, failure or poor performance at school, a family or social crisis, a fight with a boyfriend or girlfriend, feeling lonely, isolated, depressed or confused.

All adolescents in recovery will experience emotionally difficult times. Identifying and talking about these difficult times may be all it takes to deter many teens from using when difficulties exist. When these events seem intolerably painful to adolescents, the challenge to the professional is to assist the teens in lowering their anxiety and decreasing their emotional pain to a tolerable level so the adolescent can get through the immediate situation without using. Let us not forget what poor problem-solvers many of these adolescent are. The most simple solutions may not occur to them when they are in crisis. The following examples demonstrate this point.

Jim, a sixteen-year-old adolescent male come to aftercare and reported that he had used pot the day before, after two months of abstinence. At first he could not identify that anything significant had happened which contributed to his slip. As the group began asking him questions about school, he became increasingly more agitated. He denied that anything special had happened at school; in fact, he stated that he did not care what happened at school because he planned to drop out. Upon further questioning, the adolescent told the group that he was failing several subjects. Jim told the group he could do the work if he tried and that he was failing because he did not care.

This is a typical statement from addicted teens who have trouble academically. It is easier on the ego to say they do not care as opposed to acknowledging that they are trying and are failing. The teen's behavior indicated he was putting forth an effort at school. He was going to class and studying for tests. Instead of badgering the teen into admitting that he was trying and failing, the counselor directed the group and the teen to problem solve by asking them, "Even though Jim is failing because he does not care about school, suppose someone in Jim's position was failing and they did care about it. What could they try to get their grades up?" The group, as well as Jim and the counselor, were able to identify several things that could be done to try and improve the situation. By the end of group, expanded options were there for Jim to utilize if he chose to do so. Although Jim never acknowledged that he was concerned about his grades, the counselor discovered that he had taken some of the group's recommendations and did improve his academic performance enough that he passed most of his classes.

The following provides an example of an adolescent using marijuana following a significant emotional crisis which he felt ill-prepared to handle. Ted reported to his aftercare group that he had gotten drunk on his fourteenth birthday. Initially, the counselor assumed Ted had just gotten drunk to celebrate this special occasion. As Ted began answering the questions being asked, it became obvious that something else was going on. Ted stated that his birthday had come and gone with no word from his biological father. Ted's parents were divorced and he had not seen much of his father since the divorce. He had gotten in touch with his father and had talked with him while he was in treatment. Ted interpreted this lack of contact from his father as meaning that his father did not want to have anything to do with him. He also assumed that his father was feeling that Ted was still a trouble-making drug addict despite all the changes Ted was trying to make.

It is important to remember that adolescents make many assumptions about the painful things that happen to them. The assumptions are usually negative, self-degrading and not always accurate. Although the counselor did not know why Ted's father had neglected to contact him, it was obvious that Ted's assumptions, accurate or not, were creating a great deal of emotional pain for Ted. The counselor felt that in order to assist Ted in alleviating the pain, she needed an accurate assessment of the situation. She suggested that the group accompany Ted to the office phone while he called his father. Ted reached his father and discovered that the situation was not as it had initially appeared.

Ted's father informed him that he had intended to contact Ted and had discussed this with Ted's mother. Ted's mother had dissuaded the father from initiating this contact by telling Ted's father that contact from him would be disruptive to Ted and could possibly interfere with Ted's recovery. The father wanted to support Ted's efforts in recovery and had decided not to call. This phone call reduced Ted's pain and his desire to use was reduced to the point that Ted was able to leave the group, confident in his ability to continue in recovery. Alleviating or reducing the emotional or psychological pain created by social or emotional stressors enough that the adolescent does not feel the urge to use because of them is a critical step in preventing continued slips and a possible slide into relapse.

Every addicted adolescent has a deeply ingrained individualized denial system which is activated prior to a slip. The next question is crucial in assisting the teen to recognize what this denial system is, how it works, and when it was activated.

Teens cannot go from believing they are not addicted to using the drug without first rationalizing their use. In order to determine how they rationalized their slips, adolescents must answer the question, **"What did you tell yourself to make it okay to use again?"**

The cognitive messages that the teen gave himself prior to the use of the chemicals are the messages which rationalized the use and gave the teen permission to slip. It is important that the teen recognize and accept responsibility for these messages. By recognizing these messages, the teen develops a cognitive awareness of his or her delusional thinking. The teen must learn that this thinking is a sign of danger in recovery and must learn to recognize that it is a signal that something is wrong in the recovery process. This awareness makes the adolescent less vulnerable to the denial that accompanies addictions and increases their ability to avoid slips.

When teens are asked to identify this thought process, it not unusual for them to respond that they do not remember what they were thinking immediately before they began using. If this is the case, the counselor can implement the following technique to assist them in remembering.

The teen is instructed to reenact the using situation in the form of a role play. In order to make this as realistic as possible, the teen needs to recall specifically the details of the situation by remembering where the use occurred and describing the environment in detail. For example: What did the room look like? How was it set up? What color was the furniture? Utilizing all the senses will make the situation more realistic to the adolescents. What were the noises in the background? If music was playing, what song do you remember? What smells do you recall? Finally, it is important to have the players in place.

Who was there? What were they wearing? What was their role in the slip?

Once the teen has accurately set the stage, have him direct the scenario by instructing group members and assigning them specific roles. The teen will continue with this reenactment up to the point when he or she is ready to place the chemical in his/her mouth. At this time, the counselor needs to stop the teen and ask, "What is going through your head?" The thoughts are, in fact, the rationalization the teen used to justify taking the chemical. It needs to be pointed out that these thoughts are the teens "stinking thinking" and that the adolescent has two choices when the rationalization starts. He can recognize the insanity of this thinking and tell someone or he can believe his own druggy thinking and relapse.

The sixth question is designed to assist the adolescent in further assessing the relapse dynamic, which in turn works to prevent future relapse. It also lays the groundwork for the next series of questions. **The question very simply asks the teen to evaluate the recovery program and assess what, it anything, is missing.** Adolescents may be able to identify that they have not been working the twelve steps, have ignored their daily schedule, have been collecting resentments, have lost touch with their sponsor or are feeling lonely and isolated. This question is one which increases teens' awareness of their situation and identifies possible problems in their program which may need to be addressed to prevent further relapse.

The seventh question asks teens to identify how they feel "right now." One needs to be prepared for many possible answers. Most teens feel guilty or disappointed in themselves. They may feel relieved that they have shared their slip with someone.

Many teens feel that they were disappointed in the slip because the high did not provide them with the euphoria or the escape which they anticipated. Many teens will express fear because of their vulnerability. Teens may also be left in a state of confusion about their recovery. While slips for many teens provide the motivation they need to recommit to their recovery, slips for some teens only serve to strengthen their ambivalence about their recovery and increase their denial of their addiction. It is at this point that many teens make an active decision to give up on recovery and return to using. Whatever feelings teens have, it is important that these feelings be expressed openly and honestly.

The final question demands that teens take action and make a commitment one way or the other. The question is, **"What do you want to do now?"** It is important that adolescents be held accountable to answering this question with rigorous honesty. Many teens will be tempted to give the "right answer."—the answer which they perceive will meet the approval of their group members and adults and the answer which guarantees that everyone will get off their backs. At first, most teens will say they want to get back on track with their recovery program. In reality, the teen will decide to do one of three things:

1. They will, in fact, decide to get back on track with their program. In such cases, they are willing to develop a plan based on the information they have obtained by processing the slip. These are teens who will make an effort to follow the plan and make necessary changes to try and prevent further relapse. These are teens who remain in recovery because they continue to strive to maintain abstinence.

2. The teens will decide to give up on striving to maintain abstinence. They will spend a great deal of time and energy trying to figure out ways to control their use. They will tell you they want to stay in recovery, but they do not mean this and therefore, are reluctant to commit to a plan to prevent further relapse. If they do make a verbal commitment to a relapse prevention plan, their behavioral follow-through is weak or nonexistent. These are teens who are no longer in recovery but are in the early phases of active relapse.

3. The teens will decide they do not want to continue in recovery and they will openly acknowledge this. These are also teens who are in the early phases of active relapse. Teens who are in active relapse need to be removed from the recovery group and the process of relapse intervention needs to begin.

Teens who are striving to maintain abstinence, despite slips, should remain in the recovery group.

When teens answer this last question, they need to be held accountable to being honest. They need to know that recovery is always their choice and they need permission to let others know if they do not plan to continue. It is important not to accept a pat and easy answer in response to this question, as the answer will strongly influence what needs to happen next with the teen.

When this format is followed, slips can be highly therapeutic for teens. Adolescents will come away with an understanding of their own personal relapse dynamic, a plan to address their immediate stressors, a plan for strengthening the weak parts of their recovery program, and hope that they can continue from here. By processing the slip in this way, adolescents also learn a systematic method for evaluating what is going on with them so that they can learn to self-monitor and not depend solely on others to step in and intervene.

CHAPTER

8

UTILIZING TRIGGERS AS A RELAPSE PREVENTION TOOL

Professionals who work in adolescent treatment environments will recognize the following scenario. A group of adolescents are enjoying free time in their day room. They are smoking cigarettes, working on a jigsaw puzzle, visiting with one another, and listening to tunes on the radio. A popular song by a favorite group fills the room and the adolescents exchange secret glances. The counselor quickly paces across the room and nervously changes the station, recognizing that the song is a party tune that many of the adolescents associate with getting high. The counselor recognizes that for the brief time that the adolescents listened to the music, they experienced euphoric recall and a desire to get high. In fact, if given a choice at that particular time, many of the adolescents would choose to get high.

This awareness makes the counselor nervous and he/she reminds him/herself to talk to the head of the unit tomorrow about banning the radio from the treatment center altogether to avoid such situations in the future. Although the counselor does not acknowledge this to anyone, the adolescents' response to the music has increased the counselor's anxiety by increasing his awareness that many of the adolescents have not resolved their ambivalence about giving up their mood-altering chemicals. This awareness discourages the counselor and makes him/her feel that good treatment is not happening. It reminds the counselor of all the patients who have been through treatment and who have relapsed. As is frequently the case in working with adolescents, the counselor responds to this uncomfortable situation by trying to exert control over the teens.

Banning music will not address the issue of the adolescents' ambivalence about recovery, but it will make the counselor feel more in control of the situation. The situation has presented the counselor with a highly therapeutic moment, but this moment has been lost due to the counselor's anxiety and need to control. In order for treatment to be successful, we need to become skilled at utilizing therapeutic moments to assist the teens in resolving their ambivalence about recovery and to address the critical treatment issues of dealing effectively with trigger stimuli such as favorite party tunes.

One of the primary reasons for adolescent relapse is the failure of adolescents to make the appropriate and necessary lifestyle changes which promote recovery following the completion of treatment. In an effort to demonstrate the importance of recovering lifestyles, treatment centers have removed drug symbols from their environment. Treatment centers demand that adolescents give up music, dress, language and all other symbols which are related to the drug culture. Adolescents are required to cut off relationships with drug using peers and are discouraged from swapping "war stories" which glamorize their addiction. These directions work well for the handful of adolescents who are willing to do anything it takes to achieve recovery. For the majority of adolescents, it creates a power struggle and the focus becomes control between staff and patients as opposed to recovery. The adolescents openly reject what professionals tell them about lifestyle changes or comply by verbalizing intents to change without truly understanding why these changes need to take place. Creating a supportive and recovery-focused treatment environment is an essential element of treatment and we cannot allow the treatment culture to be contaminated by drug symbols. However, completely isolating adolescents from drug symbols and stimuli which trigger drug hunger serves to hamper, not enhance the treatment experience.

As opposed to ignoring triggers, we need to learn to use them as a therapeutic tool.

When we refer to the word "triggers" we are referring to people, places, things, events and emotional states which create a desire in the chemically dependent person to use a mood-altering substance. The longer the adolescent is exposed to the drug culture, the more they become conditioned to respond to drug stimuli. As we have learned from working with cocaine addicted individuals, understanding and learning to manage triggers which result in drug hunger is an essential component to recovery and relapse prevention. Unfortunately, we frequently ignore this information when working with addicted teens. It is time for treatment professionals to recognize the importance and the therapeutic wisdom of using exposure to triggers and drug stimuli as a relapse prevention technique with adolescents.

PROVIDING EDUCATION
ABOUT TRIGGERS

Adolescents need to understand fully the role of triggers in relapse prevention. Experiencing drug dreams and urges to use are often frightening for adolescents. They need to understand that these are a normal part of early recovery, that they will experience urges to use well into the first year of recovery, that it is okay to talk to others about urges to use, and that they will not be judged because of this. Each time adolescents experience a craving to use and do not act on these cravings, it enhances their recovery and increases their confidence that they will be able to experience drug hunger without using once they leave the treatment environment. As adolescents continue to remain drug free, the cravings will reduce in frequency and intensity. By surviving episodes of drug hunger, adolescents begin to understand that craving states are temporary and will pass in time. It is the role of the counselor to educate adolescents about these facts. It is erroneous to assume that adolescents will be able to make these deductions or come to these conclusions without some assistance. Continued education and discussion of drug cravings and trigger responses are an essential component of treatment.

IDENTIFYING AND MANAGING EMOTIONAL AND ENVIRONMENTAL TRIGGERS

As adolescents begin to identify and understand triggers, they are able to manage their drug cravings. Emotional and behavioral management of drug hunger is one of the most valuable tools that adolescents can use to combat relapse. As one adolescent patient stated, "Learning about triggers was like having extra weapons to put in my arsenal to help me fight the battle against my addiction."

Understanding drug triggers and managing responses to these triggers is a two step process. The first step in this process is to assist the adolescent in thoroughly understanding environmental as well as emotional triggers. This is accomplished in several ways. The adolescent first needs to receive accurate and honest information about what triggers and drug hunger are and why they occur. This information must then be individualized to each adolescent to assist them in understanding which things are likely to serve as triggers for them. There may be many potential triggers that adolescents will experience outside the treatment setting that they will not experience in the treatment setting. If adolescents are not prepared for these trigger responses, they are often taken by surprise and more vulnerable to relapse.

For example, an adolescent has adopted the ritual of getting high every morning before going to school. If the adolescent is in inpatient treatment, they may wake up several mornings and never experience the urge to get high. Much to the adolescent's surprise, the first morning after discharge, he wakes up and experiences powerful urges to use. The trigger in this situation is getting ready to return to school. If adolescents are aware that this might happen, they will be more likely to deal with this in a constructive manner. If they are taken by surprise, they may very well return to drug use as a result.

In an effort to assist adolescents in completely understanding high-risk times, it is important to listen carefully to individual drug histories and to listen for cues. When listening to drug histories, assist the adolescents in identifying which times during the day were most tied to drug use. These times frequently include waking up in the morning, lunch, directly after school, and bedtime. Times that have traditionally been first use of the day are often the strongest triggers for teens.

Explain to the adolescents that when they first experience these events following treatment they should not be surprised if the events trigger powerful urges to use. Other techniques can be employed to assist adolescents in thoroughly exploring possible anxiety-producing situations which may create drug hunger. One mechanism for doing this is to develop a trigger checklist. The best way to develop this list is to identify several different categories such as social situations, romance, school or work situations, celebrations, music, TV, movies, ads, recreational activities, and people, places or things which might trigger urges to use. This completed list will probably be several pages long. Have each patient carefully go through his list and identify the top ten trigger situations. Each patient then shares his list with the group which assists him in identifying which situations can be avoided and which situations cannot be avoided. For example, adolescents can avoid parties where others are using, but they cannot always avoid school situations which are related to using.

Each patient is then asked to develop a three-part strategy for dealing with the triggers which cannot be avoided. Once strategies have been developed, the teens can practice implementing them through the use of role play. These strategies are then incorporated into the adolescent's relapse prevention plan. Working on triggers in treatment is an ongoing process that takes a considerable amount of time. The suggested techniques may take several group sessions to complete. Working on environmental triggers is a task that can begin early in an inpatient or hospital program, soon after the adolescent has completed a detox and initial adjustment period. In outpatient treatment, trigger management begins immediately.

Once the adolescent has developed some understanding of and skill in dealing with environmental triggers, the identification and management of emotional triggers can be addressed. Chemically dependent adolescents enter treatment with a long history of avoiding feelings by medicating them through drug use. During the process of becoming addicted, they have failed to develop skills in identifying and coping productively with emotions. Consequently, certain emotions trigger the urge to use chemicals. The adolescents frequently do not understand the connection between their urges to use and their emotions, particularly during the early weeks of recovery. Helping the adolescent understand their emotional triggers can be accomplished in several ways.

Retrospective evaluation of the urges which the adolescent experiences throughout the day is one mechanism which can be used. For example, when the adolescents discuss a particularly strong urge to use, they first need to identify the environmental trigger for that urge. Secondly, they need to evaluate and identify the emotional trigger. The emotional trigger can be identified by encouraging the adolescent to discuss the incident which precipitated the urge and to talk about any emotions or feelings that were present during that incident. It may be helpful to have the adolescent keep a log in which they record (1) when they experienced cravings, (2) what the situation was, and (3) what the emotion was. In reviewing this log with their group, counselor or sponsor, patterns will quickly begin to emerge. It will become evident that adolescents experience urges to use around particular emotions such as anger, conflict, or feeling embarrassed or lonely. Once the teens are able to identify those emotions, the feelings will no longer create such an urge to use.

Another technique which is helpful is to encourage the adolescent to identify urges which surface during particularly emotional therapy sessions or when conflict arises and is addressed during the course of treatment. For example, during particularly emotional group or family therapy sessions it is not unusual to see that an adolescent patient seems to have emotionally "checked out." When this occurs, it is important to take time out to ask the adolescent if he is experiencing urges to use and what the precipitating emotion was. By providing adolescents with a mechanism to identify and discuss their feelings, they are being taught alternatives to using in order to medicate these feelings. In addition, their level of confidence in their ability to experience and successfully handle uncomfortable emotions increases as does their faith in themselves and their ability to remain chemically free.

When treating dual diagnosed adolescents, understanding emotional triggers is critical. Many dual diagnosed adolescents do not understand the connection between their psychiatric diagnosis and their use of mood-altering chemicals. By utilizing the previously outlined technique, counselors can help these adolescents realize that they often use to medicate their feelings of depression, anxiety or hyperactivity. This serves to reinforce for the adolescent their need to follow the prescribed course of treatment for their psychiatric diagnosis.

CHAPTER
9

UTILIZING TRIGGERS AS A
METHOD OF REDUCING DENIAL

Adolescents frequently choose not to make recovery-focused lifestyle changes during treatment because they do not develop an acceptance of their powerlessness over drugs during the treatment experience. They may maintain that they have control over their use, or that they will be able to associate with old friends and go to old hangouts because they truly believe they will not be affected or influenced by their surroundings. Most adolescents leave treatment with the unverbalized belief that they will be able to use the knowledge they have gained in treatment to help them "control" their use of mood-altering chemicals. They believe that they can go to parties where chemicals are being used and that they can associate with old drug-using peers because they have no appreciation for the powerful drug hunger they will experience in these situations. Counselors often become very frustrated and remark that they have told these kids a thousand times that they cannot hang around with using peers. Unfortunately, adolescents do not learn by being told what to do by adults.

The best way for adolescents who are stuck in denial to understand their powerlessness is to experience that powerlessness and loss of control during the treatment experience. This can be easily accomplished in outpatient treatment where the teen is continually struggling with these issues. However, young addicts cannot experience that powerlessness in a treatment environment where all the triggers which represent the drug culture have been removed.

The most potent therapy sessions I have ever conducted with addicted teens in a treatment environment were precipitated by the adolescents' exposure to drug stimuli. They were exposed to excessive drinking by others during a holiday pass, or wandered by a liquor store on their way to a therapeutic recreational activity. These experiences stirred strong desires to use and provided the patients with an opportunity to develop a true understanding of their loss of control over their chemicals. This significantly impacted their denial.

Structured and controlled exposure to drug stimuli which serve as triggers for addicted teens is a powerful therapeutic technique which plays an integral part in assisting teens in working through their denial. This exposure can take many forms. For example, providing staff lead activities in which teens are allowed to listen to music or watch movies which discuss or show individuals using chemicals frequently results in teens experiencing strong urges to use. When observing the teens' response to exposure to drug stimuli, several things may happen.

The adolescents' posture and mannerisms may change as the teens revert back to old drug-using stances and attitudes. The teens may experience physical changes such as increased heart rate, perspiring, and trembling hands. When this occurs, it is important to stop the activity, ask the teens to explain what is going on with them physically and emotionally, give them feedback on what you have observed, and point out to them that this is why they need to change playmates and playgrounds upon leaving treatment.

If teens experience such a strong reaction to a song or a movie, how will they respond to people using drugs around them, a party atmosphere or friends talking about getting high? Therapeutic opportunities such as these present themselves daily in a treatment environment when patients come to group or are admitted to the hospital while under the influence, when patients exchange war stories, when patients visit places associated with using (i.e., parks, bowling alleys, or arcades), or when patients see drug-related symbols such as T-shirts and paraphernalia. When these therapeutic opportunities present themselves, they must be utilized as treatment tools as opposed to being ignored or controlled. These activities allow teens to experience their powerlessness as opposed to talking about powerlessness. Exposure to triggers is the best way for teens to learn that certain people, places, and things which have always been associated with drug use will trigger urges to use and therefore, need to be eliminated from the adolescent's lifestyle. This technique is more effective than merely telling the teens why they have to make the changes we are demanding of them.

Similarly, exposure to powerlessness can be extremely helpful in breaking through a particularly resistant adolescent's denial. One technique which is helpful when dealing with resistant patients is known as "allowing the patient to encounter his or her drug of choice." This experiential activity is conducted by selecting two group members who will place their chairs facing one another in the middle of the group circle. The resistant patient is told he will be having a conversation with his/her drug of choice. The second group member will be instructed to play the drug and attempt to seduce his partner. Adolescents are frequently extremely skilled at playing a line of coke, a bag of pot or a beer. They may not need to be coached, but if they are faltering, coach them to focus on the promised feeling or reward, the anticipation and the rituals. What frequently happens is that resistant teens who adamantly maintain they have no problem with their chemical use, will be easily seduced by the drug. They will lean forward in their chairs, their hands may tremble, their eyes become wide open, their heart rate increases and their faces turn red. All this is accompanied by a powerful and overwhelming desire to get high.

When it is evident that the adolescent is experiencing a strong urge, stop the encounter and make full therapeutic use of this highly anxiety-filled time. Ask the resistant teens to describe how they feel, what they notice physically, and the intensity of their cravings. Ask other group members to give feedback on physical responses and changes they noticed. Ask the teens directly if they would use if they had a choice at that moment. While the teens' anxiety is high, point out that this is what we mean by powerlessness. That exposure to and thought of the chemical creates a cunning, baffling and powerful response that is beyond their control. Allowing teens to experience this powerlessness and feel uncomfortable with it often serves as a turning point for them in the recovery process.

It is important to take adequate time to process this activity by allowing each person in the group to discuss their response to the role play. Many people in the group will experience urges to use and will have an opportunity to practice some of the strategies they have developed for managing drug hunger.

It is important to make certain that the teens' anxiety has been lowered before they leave the room. It is also important to monitor which teens participate in this activity.

Teens who are in their first week of treatment or who are struggling with detox should not participate. Dually diagnosed adolescents who are not psychiatrically stabilized need to be carefully screened before participating in such activities. Addicted adolescents who are particularly sensitive to anxiety (i.e., teens with borderline tendencies, anxiety or panic disorders, or teens who are manic or schizophrenic) may not be appropriate candidates for such an activity. However, addicted adolescents who are depressed, or who present with conduct disorders or oppositional defiant disorders, may benefit greatly from this type of activity.

It is important to be aware of the anxiety produced by this activity. The activity can be easily sabotaged by staff's own anxiety or their discomfort at the group's anxiety level. Counselors must realize that anxiety can be an invaluable treatment tool with highly resistant adolescents.

REFRAMING TRIGGERS

Identifying and learning to manage triggers and drug hunger by avoiding situations which stimulate cravings are important tools for adolescents in recovery. However, the technique of reframing triggers also has significant value in treating addicted teens. Reframing refers to the process of changing the context in which the teens experience the trigger, thereby having the trigger take on a new meaning to the adolescent. This is particularly important given the fact that adolescents cannot avoid all situations and places that were previously associated with their drug use.

Activities and events that are a normal healthy part of growing up may be fraught with triggers for many addicted teens. If adolescents are going to establish a recovering lifestyle that is appealing and exciting, many activities may need to be reframed for them. Recreational therapy plays an important part in this process. During the course of treatment, teens should participate in staff-lead and supervised outings that expose them to places where they used to get high. Obviously, we are not talking about encouraging kids to go to drug-using parties or to hang out at drug-users' corner at school or other places which are the adolescent equivalent of a bar. We are referring to places such as parks, arcades, ball games, sober dances, shopping malls, etc.

Once adolescents have visited these places as part of the treatment process and have remained clean and sober during the visits, these places take on new meanings. The more the activity is recovery-related, the more effective the reframing. For example, it is certainly therapeutic for recovering teens to visit a local park, have a picnic and throw a frisbee around. It is more powerful to conduct periodic group sessions in that park. By doing this, we have changed the way the park will be viewed and have made it part of the adolescents' recovery experience. These reframing activities work out well as long as they are carefully planned, well-chosen and can provide an adequate amount of structure and supervision for the teens.

One of the experiences that need to be reframed for many teens is the school environment. If adolescents are in inpatient treatment, they are usually ill-prepared for how they will feel when they return to the school building where they frequently used, bought and sold chemicals. The building itself holds many triggers that frequently take even the most motivated teen by surprise and place them at risk for relapse. More time and consideration needs to be given to helping the adolescent reframe this experience. Prior to the teens' discharge from treatment, if at all possible, they need to be allowed to visit school with a support person. They need to walk down the halls, past smokers' corner and to their locker to experience those powerful urges while they still have support to deal with these urges.

This serves to help desensitize the adolescents to the initial urges they experience upon entering the building. They will still experience urges when they return to school, but the urges will not be as strong and the teen will not be taken by surprise by them and will have had time to develop plans for dealing with them. One group of adolescents I worked with was very aware of how vulnerable recovering teens were when returning to school. When learning of a teen returning to school, they would make it a point to meet the teen at the front door, walk the teen to his locker and even arrange a schedule so that another recovering teen would be there at lunch and to walk the returning adolescent to classes throughout the day.

When working with teens in an outpatient setting, it is important to attempt to reframe the school experience very early in the treatment process. Identifying a support person to walk the adolescent through the building is a helpful technique for outpatients. If this is not possible, conducting an imaged walk-through is helpful. During this activity, simply ask the adolescents to accompany you on an imagined trip down the halls of the school. Ask them to describe the building and the process of entering the parking lot (parking lots are major triggers for some teens), entering the front door and walking down the hall. During that walk, ask them to describe any rough spots or potential trouble spots. When they arrive at a trouble spot, ask them to describe this to you and describe how they feel. Ask them to imagine walking by this spot without stopping to get stoned, and walking on to a safe place. This activity will serve to reframe the school experience as well as prepare the teens for possible trigger reactions they may encounter at school.

One of the battles treatment professionals continually struggle with and often lose is that of music. Because many adults do not like or do not understand the music of adolescents, we associate all rock music with drug use and/or satanism. Because we do not know what do to with this issue, we resort to control and ban the music from the treatment centers. The reality is that music is important to teenagers. If we want to win the music battle, we need to teach teens how to use music to enhance their recovery. Certainly, some music may need to be labeled as off limits for teens in treatment, but not all music. Many adults tell me they eliminate all rock music because they do not know and do not have time to research which music is drug-related and which is not. I would contend that if you plan to work effectively with teens, you need to take time to find out.

One method which can be used to reframe music is to do a lecture or workshop which I call "Music for Recovery" (White, 1990.) The workshop is conducted in the following manner: Tell the group they can select three of their favorite songs to listen to in this activity. Inevitably, the group will bring the most forbidden music they can find. Ask them to make sure you have copies of the lyrics to pass out to the group. Allow the teens to listen to their songs and process what effect the music has on their mood, attitude, behavior, etc. Begin the process of reframing by turning off the music and reviewing the lyrics line by line. In reviewing the lyrics, the group is asked to compare the message of the music to the reality of the drug lifestyle. This is easy to do since many rock stars whose songs promoted drug use are now recovering or have sought treatment. It is valuable to point out to teens that if the messages of glamour and fun in the music were indeed true, then why have so many of these stars decided to give up their chemical use? Once this workshop is completed, the music takes on a completely different meaning for the adolescent. This is not a guarantee that the teens will stop listening to this music, but the activity has changed the way they experience this music.

During the second part of the workshop, the therapist picks three songs and asks the teens to listen to them and review the lyrics. In order for this activity to be successful the therapist must pick music that reflects the teens' taste. The therapist many need to spend time reviewing lyrics on album covers to find lyrics that can have a recovery-related meaning. After the songs have been played, the lyrics are reviewed and their recovery-related message is identified. This is followed by a discussion of ways in which teens can use music to enhance their recovery.

One group of recovering young people who were participants in an aftercare group which I led were very tied into music. This particular group of teens had a high recovery rate largely due to their creativity and determination to have fun in the recovery process. They decided they wanted to attend a rock concert in town and decided they would devise a way to do this so that their recovery would not be jeopardized. Against my adamant protest and projections that they would relapse if they pursued this, they proceeded to buy a row of tickets to be used by recovering teens only. They also set some ground rules for themselves which included precautions that stipulated that no one left the auditorium for any reason unless accompanied by another recovering teen. The teens went to the concert, greatly enjoyed themselves and did not relapse. They have been doing this for years. This has become such a popular activity that they often buy rows of tickets. These teens were able to reframe this activity successfully so they did not have to give up concert attendance in order to maintain recovery. As a result, recovery was much more attractive and appealing.

A very dramatic example of reframing is depicted in the following case scenario. A very musically talented adolescent female was admitted to inpatient treatment for her addiction to pot and alcohol. As treatment progressed, it was obvious that the adolescent was holding tightly to her drugs and was not about to let go. This puzzled the staff because this particular adolescent appeared to be a good candidate for successful treatment as she had many things working for her that would support her recovery. By closely examining the case, we discovered that the teen was being told by staff that she would have to let go of her aspirations to be a rock star if she wanted to recover from her addiction. The adolescent was convinced that the only thing she could do well was her music. Her self-esteem was tied into her music as were her future hopes and dreams. Staff were unwittingly discouraging this teen from choosing recovery by focusing on what she had to give up as opposed to what she could gain.

The staff was faced with the decision to lose the battle or use the only door that was available for reaching this teen —her music. With this realization, staff changed their game plan. The staff no longer focused on the adolescent giving up her music. Instead, they began to integrate her music into her recovery program. Some of the traditional rules of the treatment center were challenged and changed as the team realized that engaging this teen in recovery was more important than some of the traditional rules, such as not allowing musical instruments in treatment. She was allowed to bring her keyboard into treatment with the understanding that she could only play or write recovery-related music. They also had her read life stories of several recovering rock stars.

Staff members were particularly touched one day during a parent visitation when the adolescent played a song that she had written to express her appreciation to her father for his support. The adolescent often expressed her feelings and struggles with recovery through her music. The staff was successful in assisting this teen in reframing a behavior that was previously drug-related into a behavior which was recovery-related. The adolescent has been involved in a successful recovery program for several years. She has also actively pursued her musical career. In all likelihood, this recovery would not have been possible if staff had not been skilled at reframing.

CHAPTER

10

RELAPSE INTERVENTION

In spite of our best efforts at relapse prevention, there will be some adolescents who will make the decision not to continue in recovery. Teens who are no longer striving to maintain abstinence from mood-altering chemicals are teens who are in relapse. It is critical when working with adolescents to be able to determine which teens are slipping and which teens are in relapse. Once a professional has determined the adolescent is in relapse, the clinical approach shifts from one of a relapse prevention mode to a relapse intervention mode. The goals of relapse prevention are to interrupt or prevent patterns of use while the goals of intervention are to determine how to use the relapse in a therapeutic manner. Because the goals are so different, the relapsed adolescent should be removed from the recovery group and placed in a relapse intervention group or seen individually.

If the relapsed teen remains in a recovery-oriented group, the group will be adversely affected by the relapsed teen's dishonesty, refusal to change and denial. The recovery group may lose focus and productivity as it becomes more and more preoccupied with the relapsed teen's chemical use. In addition, the relapsed teen will sabotage the efforts of the group and its leaders. Finally, the recovery group is not productive for the adolescent in active relapse. Eventually, the relapsed teen will drop out or be kicked out of the group. The group and the counselor will feel somewhat relieved because they did not know what else to do. Unfortunately, this is not helpful to the adolescent or the family.

There is another alternative that is designed to get as much therapeutic mileage as possible out of the relapse process. This five-step relapse intervention model is outlined in detail in the following pages. It is important to bear in mind that anywhere in this process the adolescent may shift from a relapse mode back into a recovery mode.

STEP ONE: Decide when rehospitalization or readmission to treatment will be therapeutically best for the adolescent. We have, as a profession, been guilty of prematurely rehospitalizing adolescents who have relapsed. We are uncomfortable with the fact that they have returned to using mood-altering substances and respond to this by readmitting to treatment before the adolescent is ready to benefit from another treatment experience. As a result, the adolescent has no motivation for recovery and we perpetuate that revolving door of treatment that yields very poor results. The challenge is to work with the relapse process in order to make it therapeutic.

Working with the relapse process includes waiting until the adolescent experiences some type of motivational crisis before readmitting the adolescent to treatment. In order for this crisis to occur, we must allow the adolescent to experience the pain and negative consequences of the relapse. We must refrain from jumping in and saving him/her from the consequences of his/her use. This is a difficult position for the therapist who feels pressure from parents, courts and schools to do something with this teen. We must be confident that by following the relapse intervention model outlined in this chapter, we are following the most appropriate clinical course for the teen. We are working to make sure the relapse has a therapeutic impact on this young person and we are not rescuing the young person from this impact.

We frequently want to rush to readmit the adolescent after they have experienced a certain number of slips or when we first recognize that they have made a decision to return to drug use. We must remember that when teens initially return to using, they are able to maintain some level of control over their use. This control reinforces their denial that they are not addicted and they sincerely believe they will be able to use without experiencing negative consequences. If teens are hospitalized or forced into an intense level of treatment at this point, at the very peak of their denial, the intervention is a total waste. Their denial at this point is almost impenetrable. They sit in treatment and may be very compliant, but are totally convinced they have control over their use. They are frequently very clever at saying whatever they need to say to get through treatment as quickly and painlessly as possible. At this point, the length and intensity of treatment does not make a difference. The only way to penetrate the denial is to allow the teen to lose control over their use; this cannot be accomplished while the adolescent is in inpatient treatment.

To readmit an adolescent to treatment prematurely is not only counter-therapeutic, but also enabling. This was clearly demonstrated to me in the following case. A fifteen-year-old female was a favorite of the treatment staff. She was a good candidate for success and the treatment team liked her very much. She left treatment and experienced some episodes of use about which she was not honest. Three months after her discharge from treatment, the treatment center received a call in the middle of the night from the local police. The adolescent had relapsed, taken her mother's car, and had been picked up by the police. She begged the police and her parents to let her go back into treatment to avoid legal charges. The police called the treatment center and informed them that the adolescent could return to treatment or go to jail. If she returned to treatment, charges would not be filed. The very caring treatment team quickly decided that treatment was the best option. A few days after this incident, I was giving the parent lecture on enabling. It occurred to me that we had indeed enabled this teen. We taught her that she could use treatment to avoid responsibility for her use and her decisions. We had protected her from the pain and consequences of her relapse. We had rescued her from what might have been a motivational crisis. It became apparent to me that the adolescent would probably remain very compliant in treatment without making any changes.

Two months after the adolescent was discharged from her second treatment experience, the treatment center received a call. Once again, it was the local police who explained that this same adolescent had relapsed on cocaine and had threatened to attack her mother with a knife. Her options were to go back to treatment or go to jail and have charges filed. The police were told that the adolescent would not be accepted back into treatment that time. The treatment center recommended she go to jail, face her legal charges and receive a sentence. Once that was done, if she still wanted back into treatment, she could call. The adolescent ended up with three subsequent arrests and a psychiatric hospitalization before calling about being readmitted to treatment. When her pain was severe enough, she pursued treatment. She has been clean and sober for several years now. She made that decision only after others stopped enabling and rescuing her.

Herein lies one of the major differences between adolescent relapsers and adolescents who have not had previous treatment. For adolescents with no previous treatment experience, the most helpful thing to do might be to give them the choice between jail and treatment. For adolescent relapsers, the dynamics are different and so is the course of action. Deciding when it will be therapeutically best to rehospitalize the adolescent depends on the adolescent. In most situations, adolescents need to be allowed to experience a crisis. What constitutes a crisis for one teen does not constitute a crisis for another. For some adolescents, failing a class might mean a crisis; for others, being arrested does not phase them. Addicted adolescents who have a co-existing psychiatric diagnosis such as depression may experience a crisis more quickly than an addicted teen who does not have a psychiatric diagnosis. The therapist must work with families, courts, and schools to determine what crisis to anticipate. This is an important part of the intervention process that is known as networking and will be discussed later in this chapter.

Individuals inevitably ask, "What if the adolescent's use is so bad that they become suicidal?" An adolescent who is suicidal is in crisis and is, therefore, appropriate for readmission to treatment. Professionals also ask, "What is our liability if we know the adolescent is using? "If something happens to them are we negligent?" The answer is that we are not liable for patients who continue to drink or use. Treatment in most states is "voluntary" and cannot be forced unless there is evidence that the adolescent is homicidal or suicidal. We must address the underlying anxiety behind these questions. Working with teens in relapse is difficult and anxiety-producing. It is easier for everyone involved to readmit the adolescent to treatment. The question which must be answered is—What is best for the adolescent?

Programs for addicted teens must have very strict readmission policies for teens who have relapsed. If a teen is struggling with slips and is unable to get back on track, a brief readmission to inpatient treatment might be appropriate if intensive outpatient treatment has not been successful. However, an adolescent who has relapsed and who has not experienced any anxiety about this relapse, is not appropriate for inpatient readmission. In most cases, relapsed teens are not ready for readmission for at least six months following a return to use. It is, however, more important to consider the extent to which their relapse has progressed and the number of crises it has created when determining appropriateness as opposed to merely counting months. It is also important to note that inpatient treatment is not always the best treatment options for these teens. Relapsed teens who display even a little motivation for recovery are excellent candidates for intensive outpatient programs.

STEP TWO: Determine that the adolescent is in relapse. It is critical in this step for adolescents to acknowledge that they have made a decision to return to active use of chemicals and that they are no longer striving to maintain abstinence. The manner in which this is approached with teens is very important. Teens will not admit at this point that they are in relapse. After all, relapse is for people who have a real problem. At this point, the denial is so intense that they are convinced they can use without losing control. The goal for the professional is to get teens to acknowledge their use openly and talk about the thinking that surrounds the use. The goal here is not to "talk the teen" or "confront the teen" back into recovery. This may be a difficult shift for professionals to make. We often expect that at the end of our sessions, we have done a good job if we have persuaded the teen to return to recovery. This is an unrealistic goal at this point in the relapse process.

It is important to remember that teens in recovery do not give up on recovery without having given it serious thought. The thinking process may be distorted, but none the less, the teens have thought about it. The first part of this step in the intervention is simply to say to the teen, "You know, I have been thinking a lot about this and it seems to me that you have made a decision not to continue in the program. I believe you have made a decision to return to using chemicals. What do you think?"

The question has to be phrased in a very nonjudgmental, matter-of-fact manner. I intentionally avoid using the word "relapse" because teens will become defensive and shut down communication. Relapse implies failure and it also implies to them that they are addicted, which they do not believe to be true at this stage of the game. Most teens will acknowledge that they have made a decision to return to using, but they will deny that they have relapsed. The goal is to give the teen permission to tell you that they have, in fact, made this decision.

If the professional has the type of relationship with the teen that is based on honesty, this part of the intervention should be fairly simple. Most teens will tell you that you are correct. If the teen denies this, the next step is to tell him/her why you believe this with a statement such as, "Let me tell you why I think this..." The counselor then lists the signs that indicate that the teen has given up on recovery. These things frequently include not attending meetings, frequent use, dishonesty about use, and continued slips without any effort to make the changes necessary to avoid future slips. Once again, the approach is very non-confrontational. The message to the teen needs to be that you are not particularly invested in hearing that the teen wants to return to recovery. I have often made statements such as, "Look, recovery is a personal choice. You always have the choice to return to use. The important thing to me now is that you just level with me about what type of choice you have made." At this point, the teen will usually become honest and admit that they have made a decision to return to using.

It is important that the counselor avoid the impulse to try and convince the teen that they are making a poor choice, confront them about the negative consequences of their use, or try to get the adolescent to verbally re-commit to recovery. All of these interactions will stop the process and result in the teen telling you whatever you want to hear just to get you off his or her back. The counselor then needs to move into the next step in the intervention process.

STEP THREE: Clarify the adolescent delusional system. The adolescent has obviously made the decision to return to use through delusional thinking. The counselor should begin to explore, define, and expose this delusional thinking. In order to be effective, this probing needs to be done in a very subtle way. It is not appropriate to confront the teen directly by making statements such as, "That is just your denial talking," or "You're rationalizing now." It is best to avoid such statements quite simply because they are ineffective and do not reach the teen. These statements might be effective in relapse prevention or in treatment, but not in the relapse intervention process.

The delusional system is illuminated in a more subtle manner. I frequently switch to a "Colombo" type of approach in order to get the information I need to continue this process with the client. There are two assumptions that underlie this approach. First, teens do not return to use without a plan for how they will avoid having future problems with their use and second, most teens truly believe their plan will help them maintain control over their use. Teens do not say, "I am going back to smoking pot every day so I can get busted again and flunk out of school." Instead, they tell themselves, "I know what I need to do to avoid problems. I can control my use so it will not get as bad as it was before." In order to expose the delusional thinking, the counselor must get the adolescent to identify what their plan is for controlling their use.

This is accomplished with a series of questions. The first question is, "Look, I know you thought a lot about this decision. I know you have decided you can control your use because I know you don't want things to go back to the way they were before. I am really interested in what you have told yourself that convinces you it is okay to use again." The teen will then reveal the rationalizations that underlie the delusional thinking. These rationalizations are very individualized and you cannot continue your work with the teen until the rationalizations are identified for you. These rationalizations may include statements such as, "I am not like the other people in AA, my use was never that bad," "I only got into real trouble when I drank, I'll be fine if I stick with the pot," "I only used because I was depressed and I am not depressed any more," "It is only a problem if I drink and drive and I have learned my lesson about that." I even had one adolescent tell me, "I was such a pot head but you know I think it will be okay if I stick with acid."

Adolescents have usually been nurturing these rationalizations in their heads. When they are unspoken, they tend to make sense to the teen. Sometimes just verbalizing these rationalizations is all teens need to recognize they are conning themselves and thinking crazy. I will frequently ask adolescents to listen closely as I repeat the rationalizations back to them and ask, "Tell me, how does that sound to you?" Teens may say that it does sound pretty stupid now that they think about it and that they are willing to work with the counselor to get back on the track in recovery. Teens may, however, say that it makes perfect sense to them and would make sense to you if you would just listen and try to understand. If this is the stance the teen takes, it is time to move on to the next step in this process.

The next part of the process is to have teens verbalize their plan for how they expect to maintain control over their use of chemicals. If adolescents are sincerely committed to their rationalizations, I then say to them, "Since I know you do not want to have the same problems with your use that you had before, and since I know you have given this a great deal of thought, I know you must have a plan for how you are going to maintain control over your use. I really would like to hear that plan." I always write down what they tell me. In writing this down, I begin what is referred to as a relapse log on the teens. Sometimes I tell them that I am very interested in this plan because if it works, it will be very helpful to all my other clients. Delusional adolescents buy into this quickly. I recently had a particularly grandiose adolescent tell me he thought that writing his plan down was a great idea. In fact, he thought we should try to get it published!

Sometimes I tell teens that I need to write the plan down because my memory is not very good. I always ask them if they mind if I write it down. The adolescents will then proceed to share their plan. The plan usually includes statements such as, "I will only use pot and not alcohol," "I will only use on week ends," "I will only use with certain people," "I will only use a certain amount," etc. Continuing in the Colombo mode, I question the holes in the plan under the guise of "I just want to make sure I understand this now," or "I just want to make sure you have all your bases covered here." I will frequently, in a confused manner, question parts of the plan with questions such as, "Now how are you going to make sure you do not get arrested for under age drinking?" "Now, didn't you try that before and it did not work? How is it going to work now?" Once again, just exploring this plan may be enough for adolescents to realize their delusional thinking. If they are convinced their plan will work, I ask the final question: "Tell me, how will you know when your drinking or drug use is getting out of control?" Most teens quickly respond with statements such as, "If I use during school—If I use pot again—If I drink more than three or four beers, etc., I will know that my use is getting bad again."

When adolescents have answered the three questions, I ask if I can read to them what I have written down just to make sure I have it right. I then proceed to read back to them what they have told me. Traditionally at this point, we have told adolescents that there is nothing else we can do for them if they have made the decision to continue to use and we discharge them from therapy. Relapse intervention requires that we get as much therapeutic mileage as possible out of the relapse episode and this requires that we continue to see the adolescent in counseling, at least for the time being.

During the next session, ask the adolescents about their drug or alcohol use during the previous week. Most teens will be honest with you since they have no reason to lie. After all, they have told you quite frankly that they plan to continue to use. It is important for them to tell you what they used, how much they have used and when they used. Compare their level of use with the plan they have established for themselves. What will likely happen is that for the first week or so, they will stick to the plan and will have very little problem doing this.

This increases their delusions about their use. Eventually, adolescents will report use that is a deviation from their plan.

When this happens, casually bring this to their attention with statement such as, "Wait a minute, you told me that one of the ways you would control your use is not to use during the week and you just told me that you got high on Thursday night." This comment is likely to be met with hostility on the part of adolescents as they rationalize their behavior with a comment such as, "Thursday night is not a week night; it is considered part of the weekend at our school." Your response should be to remark casually that you were confused and then state that you want to change this on the plan just to make sure you have it right. I once had an adolescent tell me that he would know he was out of control with his use if he used cocaine. When I confronted him with subsequent reports of cocaine use, he became indignant and told me that it didn't really count as use as long as he was snorting and not smoking it.

Once teens have deviated from the original plan, progression and loss of control happens rather quickly. Teens will report more frequent use with each visit. The therapist responds to this by continuing to modify and update the plan. It is also helpful to review periodically all the modifications that have been made in the plan since it was first developed. I often do this by saying, "Let me read to you what we have so far, just to make sure that I haven't missed anything. When we started out this is what you said and this is where we are now. Did I forget anything?" This technique outlines for adolescents their loss of control even as they verbally insist that they are maintaining control. It also serves to make them keenly aware of the extent to which they are delusional in their thinking, although it is unlikely that they will verbalize any of this to the counselor. Adolescents will later tell the therapist that they hated this process because it made them realize how much they were conning themselves about their use. This technique also clearly out lines for adolescents their own personal relapse dynamic as it is happening. This information is invaluable for teens who decide to give recovery another shot somewhere down the road.

The counselor continues to see teens until their use is out of control. When a teen's relapse has progressed to the point that the adolescent is using almost daily, using on the days sessions are scheduled, and perhaps even coming to the sessions under the influence, it is time to discontinue the sessions with the teen. Stopping the sessions is a strategic move with very specific goals. It is likely that the adolescent is reaching a crisis point in his life because of the use. It is also possible that the one steady thing he relies on is the relationship with the counselor. Ending the sessions is part of the process of creating a crisis in order to motivate the teen to seek recovery or treatment. The counselor tells the teen that the teen's use has reached a point that the counselor cannot help the teen. It is important to let the adolescent know you care about what happens to him. In fact, I frequently ask the teen to give me a call once a week just to let met know how he is doing. It is also important for adolescents to know you will be more than happy to help them if they decide to do something about their use of chemicals. Discharging the adolescent from treatment is a move that is designed to pull the rug out from under the client's feet in order to help facilitate a motivational crisis. In order for the intervention to work, it is important to understand that one cannot work with addicted teens in isolation. When working with adolescents in relapse, one must remain in close contact with parents, schools, and probation officers. Networking is an important part of the intervention process as is discussed in step four.

STEP FOUR: Network with significant others. Parents, teachers, and probation officers all play a critical part in the recovery process for adolescents. It is important not to try to work with adolescents in isolation. Isolation will sabotage any attempts to work effectively with teens in recovery. It is also important to remember to start working with the network very early in the process and not to wait until the teen has relapsed. The family and the network need to understand what you are trying to accomplish with the adolescent. As we have previously mentioned, therapists often feel pressured by parents, school officials and probation officers to do something about this teen before he/she gets into big trouble. I have often had someone in the adolescent's network refer a relapsed teen for readmission to inpatient treatment. When it was determined that the time was not right for readmission, the referring sources would become angry at me. Therapists often get responses such as, "If something does not happen soon, we are going to have to kick this kid out of school, or violate his probation, or he/she is going to fail." "What are we supposed to do?" all these well meaning people ask. The answer to that is that we are not going to protect this adolescent from any of these realities. Perhaps the adolescent needs to be kicked out of school or taken back to court in order for them realize the consequences of their addiction. The response to what do we do is simple. We do whatever the teen's behavior dictates is appropriate to do.

The counselor reinforces this approach with the family. The family at this point is usually concerned, scared and frustrated; it is to be expected that they will seek immediate relief. The counselor encourages the family to continue to hold the adolescent responsible for his behavior and not to fall back into enabling. This helps keep the adolescent's anxiety about his use high. One family that I worked with was concerned about their daughter's continuing to stay out all night. They indicated to her that when she stayed out all night, they would file a police report as well as apply other consequences to the behavior. The daughter, based on past experience, did not believe her parents would consistently follow through on this. The constant runaway reports brought the adolescent to the attention of the juvenile probation department and the courts became involved in the case. This resulted in a motivational crisis for the teen. She later told me that she could not believe her parents had outlasted her. She was totally convinced that they would eventually throw up their hands and let her relapse in peace. When her parents responded by holding her accountable, it helped facilitate a crisis that eventually led to her becoming motivated for recovery.

Parents may not have any control over the decisions their children make to use or not use, but they can certainly maintain behavioral expectations and use consequences when adolescents behave inappropriately in the home. Accountability may mean calling the police when the adolescent steals things from home, letting the school know when the teen is truant from school, talking honestly to the probation officer if the teen is violating conditions of probation, and refusing to allow the teen to drive the car if they know the teen is in relapse. Most importantly, parents must not allow themselves to get caught up in the teen's craziness to the point that parents lose control over their behavior. Parents need a great deal of support and encouragement to follow through. They may need to remain involved in a support group or with the therapist after the adolescent has been discharged from counseling.

The therapist must work closely with family members to help them understand why rehospitalizing the teen prematurely is counterproductive. The therapist needs to work with the family to establish a guideline for determining when the adolescent has reached a crisis point and is, therefore, ready for readmission to treatment. Simply negotiate this by asking the family, "When will we know it is time to readmit to treatment? How will we know that your child's behavior is out of control?" Parents are usually able to identify two or three indicators that will let them know that things are reaching a crisis point with their child. It is important to bear in mind that each adolescent is different. What constitutes a crisis for one, does not necessarily constitute a crisis for another. As I have said, for some teens, failing a class may create a crisis. For others, getting arrested may not phase them. It is, therefore, important to know the adolescent and the family well when establishing these indicators. Once these indicators are established, the therapist and the family must negotiate an agreement about what will happen when the adolescent reaches this point. The end result is usually an agreement between the family and the therapist that when the adolescent reaches this point, the parent/therapist team will work together to move toward conducting an intervention with the adolescent. The goal of the intervention will be to motivate the teen back into recovery.

While the therapist works with the family, it is important that the school and other systems such as the courts be involved in this intervention process. In order to involve others in the process, the therapist needs to call the school or the probation officer and advise them of the plan which has been established with the family. The school or court can provide further opportunities to monitor the adolescent by establishing guidelines very similar to those the family has established. The therapist may ask the school or probation officer to identify, "How will we know this teen is out of control or headed for a (legal or academic) crisis?" In order to continue to monitor this, the therapist must keep in touch with others in the network. This can be accomplished by regular phone calls or a simple arrangement by which the school agrees to contact the therapist when significant events occur that indicate the teen is headed for a crisis. It is important that the network decide how the teen will be dealt with in the meantime. For example, if the teen continues to skip school, he or she should be suspended. If the teen continues to do poor work, he or she will be allowed to fail. If the teen violates probation, he or she needs to experience legal consequences. The teen's addiction cannot be used as a means of excusing him/her from poor choices. Addiction is a disease; however, it is a disease whose recovery is based on choices. These choices have consequences and adolescents need to experience consequences when their choices lead to relapse.

The monitoring methods described in this chapter are important. They provide safety nets so that the addicted teen will be intervened upon following a crisis or a series of crises. The adolescent is being closely monitored to prevent the alcohol or drug use from progressing to the point of being potentially fatal. When teens begin to show signs of depression or possible suicide or if the drug use has reached a dangerous level, the teen is intervened upon.

STEP FIVE: The Intervention. Once the therapist has reason to believe the adolescent has experienced a motivational crisis, plans are begun to readmit the teen to treatment. Frequently, the adolescent will be the one who contacts the therapist and asks for help. If the adolescent does not initiate this contact, the therapist should work toward intervening. This can include a structured Johnson Institute style of intervention (Shaffer, 1989), or it may just require a family session in which the family and the therapist inform the adolescent that he or she will be returning to treatment and what the consequences will be if he or she refuses. It is not unusual for adolescents in relapse to protest this and attempt to manipulate their way out. However, once teens know that the adults are serious, they frequently agree under protest to cooperate.

Professionals should not be fooled by an adolescent's initial resistance. Many adolescents may outwardly resist the idea of treatment, but are secretly relieved that someone has stepped in to set limits on their self-destructive behavior. Many relapsed teens who initially protest a return to treatment are very easy to motivate once the treatment process has begun. It is important to remember that treatment can include a wide range of options from once a week counseling to psychiatric hospitalization. Treatment refers more to what happens as opposed to where it happens.

FOLLOW UP: Using The Log Once in treatment, it is important that adolescents develop a thorough understanding of their own personal relapse dynamic. They need to examine closely their failed attempts to control their use, the progression of their relapse, and the rationalization that protected them from the reality of their loss of control and convinced them they could use again without experiencing negative consequences. The therapist can assist adolescents in accomplishing this by giving them the relapse log in which the therapist documented the progression of their relapse. Adolescents can read about the progression of their use and see in black and white how they tried to rationalize their use. This can have a powerful impact on teens. It can also serve as a relapse prevention tool. When adolescents find themselves rationalizing, these rationalizations will sound familiar to them. They will realize that these rationalizations did not work before and this will assist the teen in recognizing their insane thinking.

The following case study provides an example of how the relapse intervention process can be put into action:

Tom was a sixteen-year-old male who was dependent on marijuana and was a heavy acid user. He also had a long history of depression. He had been through inpatient treatment for his depression followed by treatment for his addiction. Shortly after his first chemical dependency treatment experience, he returned to using. He experienced a motivational crisis, an acid overdose, and was readmitted to the hospital for a short stay for stabilization. He was then referred to me for ongoing counseling for his depression and for relapse prevention. After about six months of recovery time, this young man began displaying signs of relapse. He denied use for several weeks before finally acknowledging it in an individual counseling session.

Tom became honest about his recent use. He was asked what he planned to do next. He quickly said that he was ready to try to re-establish abstinence and said he planned to call his sponsor, go to meetings, and come back to counseling once per week. I was greatly relieved to hear this. However, after a few moments of reflecting on this, it occurred to me that this young man was telling me what he thought he must to get me off his case so he could use in peace. It occurred to me that Tom was in the early phases of relapse and that his use was not a slip. I switched into a relapse intervention mode and stated, "I am going to ask you an important question and I want you to think about it very hard and give me the most honest answer you can. This is important because you are the only one who can answer this question. Do you really believe you have lost control of your use again?" Tom looked down and was silent for several minutes. He looked up at me with tears in his eyes and said, "Janice, I know this is hard for you to believe, but I really do have control over it this time. I promise I do."

My next question to Tom was, "If you really believe you have control over it this time, do you have any intention of giving it up and doing all those recovery things you just told me you were going to do?" Tom quietly replied, "No, I don't see a need to do any of those things, really." "Tom," I said, "You know a lot about pot use. I know you must have some kind of plan for how you are going to control your use. Why don't you tell me what it is." Tom was more than happy to share this. "Well," he said, "I've been thinking about it a lot and I know that if I stick to pot and hang around with my using friends who aren't addicted, and don't make stupid choices about when I get high, I'll be okay. If it gets bad again, I can always quit." "That's a good point, Tom," I replied. "Tell me, how will we know that it is getting bad again?" Tom said, "That's easy. If I get high in school, if my grades go down or if I blow off work because I'm too busy getting high, then I'll know it's getting bad again." "Okay," I agreed, "and if those things happen, what does that mean and what will you be willing to do?" Tom answered, "If those things happen, then I know I am headed for trouble and that I need to get back into my recovery program."

I wrote down Tom's plan and he agreed to see me on a weekly basis and keep me posted on his use. I then contacted his family to let them know what the plan was for Tom. Tom missed his appointment the following week. The week after that, he called me in a panic and demanded that he get in to see me. When I asked him what was wrong, he informed that I must have jinxed him. He told me that everything had been going fine until he wrote down his list of how he would know things were getting out of control. He informed me that in the course of two weeks his father had found pot in his car and had taken his car away, he was fired from work for being late and his grades came out and had dropped significantly. He was so upset by these events that he started using during school and had a scary binge on the weekend. He informed me that he was ready to do whatever he needed to do to get back on track. Utilizing these intervention strategies helps to insure that the relapse has an impact on the teen and truly becomes part of the recovery process. These techniques are designed so that the relapse process helps to bring the adolescent closer to recovery and that opportunities to facilitate a crisis are not lost. Teens who go through this are often experiencing a great deal of pain as a result of their relapse and are ready to do whatever it takes to make recovery work for them. They are ready to engage in the treatment process. As with the case of Tom, timing is critical. It makes the difference between adolescents coming to the conclusion they need to make changes in their life and adolescents lying to and complying with adults.

CHAPTER

11

TREATMENT IMPLICATIONS FOR RELAPSED ADOLESCENTS

As mentioned in the introduction, relapsed adolescents who have experienced previous treatment followed by a period of time in recovery have special needs. It is often quite easy to work with teens who are participating in treatment their second or third time. They understand the treatment process and basic recovery skills. As a result, they are more cooperative and less resistant. However, since they understand the system better, they are often also more manipulative and more likely to be compliant. It has been my experience that relapsed adolescents are easy to engage in the treatment process. However, they quickly realize they are hearing the same things the second time through as they did the first time. They decide they already know this information and tend to put it on auto pilot and cruise through treatment. It is easy for them to breeze through treatment because they are often wise enough to tell the counselor whatever the counselor wants to hear. In addition, peers are often reluctant to confront these kids because these adolescents have knowledge about the program and the language which is intimidating to other adolescents. In order to meet the needs of relapsed adolescents effectively, it is important that the treatment plan be individualized. This chapter will briefly discuss treatment approaches that can be utilized with this population.

WHAT WE KNOW ABOUT ADOLESCENT RELAPSE

The following research was conducted on relapsed adolescents who were involved in their second treatment experience for chemical dependency. Profiles and interviews were completed on 52 adolescents from treatment centers in Indiana, Illinois, Iowa, North Carolina, Montana, Michigan, and North Dakota. The purpose of the research was to understand better the clinical issues presented by adolescent relapsers.

Profiles were conducted on 30 males and 22 females ranging in age from 14 to 19, with the average age being 16.5 The average age of onset use was 11. Fifty-two per cent reported alcohol as their drug of choice, 17% reported marijuana as their drug of choice, and 15% reported cocaine as their drug of choice. Fifty-nine percent of these youth lived in rural communities and 41% lived in urban communities. Of the 52 youths profiled, 38 were white, two were Hispanic, two were black, six were Native American Indians, two were Black/Hispanic, and two did not report race.

Fifty-two per cent of the adolescents reported being victims of sexual abuse, 50% reported being victims of physical abuse, 83% reported parental addiction, 21% had diagnosed learning disabilities, and 53% reported significant losses. Two adolescents were diagnosed with eating disorders, six were diagnosed with depression, four with Attention Deficit Hyperactive Disorder, six with conduct disorder, two with Bipolar Disorder and two with Schizoid Affective Disorder. This research supports the concept that adolescents who relapse are addicted teens with multiple clinical issues. The extent to which these other clinical issues contributed to the relapse process is not known; however, such clinical issues do complicate the recovery process. Because of the clinical complexities presented by these teens, they need to be treated in environments which are prepared to help them in addressing and resolving these issues.

During the interviews, adolescents were asked what they felt were the main reasons for their relapse.

Twenty-four of the adolescents reported they simply did not want to stop using, five adolescents reported they thought they could control their use, and three reported that they did not think their use was a problem. These are adolescents who had not completed their pretreatment tasks and were not ready for an abstinence-based treatment experience.

Twenty-eight adolescents reported failure to make recovering life style changes (i.e., lack of AA/NA meeting attendance, failure to change friends, no sponsor contact). Five adolescents reported they did not believe their use was a problem. Thirteen adolescents indicated that peer pressure contributed to their relapse.

This data should be considered when reading this chapter which reviews the clinical needs of adolescent relapsers. Treatment for relapsed adolescents needs to focus on the following:

- Their previous failed attempts to control their use following treatment.

- Recognizing the dynamic which lead up to and contributed to the use.

- Adequate relapse prevention planning to deal with issues such as delusional thinking and peer influence.

- Recognition and resolution of clinical issues which interfere with the young person's attempt to stay clean and sober.

It is important to determine when it is best to re-admit the relapsed adolescents to treatment.

Professionals often ask the question, "How do I know if it's appropriate to readmit the adolescent to an outpatient or inpatient treatment program?" It is important to keep in mind that relapsed adolescents may present themselves for counseling or treatment as a result of pressure they are receiving from the courts, school or their families. They may make this presentation with the idea that they will continue using and will figure out a way to do it without getting caught. As indicated previously, as long as adolescents are intent on using and convinced that they do not need to work on building a recovery program, one must work with them from a relapse intervention versus an abstinence-based treatment perspective. It has been my experience that adolescents are not ready to re-commit to recovery and work from a treatment oriented, abstinence based approach until they feel they have lost control over their use and have experienced some crisis as a result of their relapse.

Readmission into any type of abstinence-based recovery program needs to be based on the fact that the adolescent is really ready to give up the mood-altering chemical. The professional must look beyond what the adolescent says to consider the entire relapse experience. I have had adolescents tell me that they were ready to re-enter recovery when, in fact, they had no intentions of doing this. I have also had relapsed adolescents initially protest re-entering recovery only to find that this protest was very superficial and more a matter of the adolescent's pride rather than indicative of their true feelings.

The first task for the relapsed adolescent is initial stabilization.

The first task for the adolescent re-entering recovery is to design treatment goals geared at stabilization. This includes interrupting a pattern of use and providing a safe period for them to detach from their drug of choice, both physically and emotionally. When considering the best way to accomplish this goal, one must consider the drug of choice, the extent of the use, and the frequency of the use. Extensive use of alcohol, inhalants and cocaine may require an inpatient detoxification experience. When I began working with adolescents ten years ago, we often said that adolescents did not require medical detoxification. Although this continues to be the case with the majority of adolescents, use histories with relapsed adolescents are often more severe than adolescents presenting for their first treatment experience. In addition, it is important to examine the adolescent's accompanying diagnosis.

Adolescents with a history of depression or borderline personality tendencies may be emotionally more unstable and may require closer monitoring. Initial stabilization requires an accurate assessment and intervention of the psychiatric issues for dually diagnosed teens.

When attempting stabilization on an outpatient basis, it is important to focus on what the adolescent can do within the next twenty-four to forty-eight hours to insure that they do not use. A very structured plan must be devised which addresses what types of drugs the adolescent has immediately accessible to them (i.e., their stash), how they plan to get rid of this supply without making themselves vulnerable to relapse, and a calendar of all the things they need to do for the next two or three days. This initial plan should include a list of places and people that they will avoid as well as a list of places and people that can be utilized to add support for them. Treatment for relapsed teens requires heavy focus on relapse prevention activities. There are several relapse prevention tasks which will be helpful for these adolescents. First and foremost, it is important to reconnect these young people to the twelve step recovery program. Secondly, it is important to work closely with them as to understanding and managing their triggers. The techniques outlined in the trigger management chapter are very appropriate and there are several additional relapse prevention techniques which can be helpful.

1. Using a Relapse Prevention Calendar: Utilize a calendar to have the adolescents preview the next 30 days of their life. During that time period, have them identify high-risk situations that might be occurring within the next month. Standard high-risk situations include Homecoming, the prom, holiday parties, spring break, etc. In addition to the standard high-risk situations, adolescents have individual high-risk situations. For example, a young man I was recently working with identified one of his high-risk situations as his older brother returning home from college for the summer. This brother was a pot smoker. The young man's return for the summer always created additional stress and anxiety on the family. Once the adolescents have identified these potential high-risk situations, they need to develop specific techniques for how they plan to deal with the situations. It is important to teach adolescents that they need to repeat this process at the end of every month.

2. Planning The Relapse: When planning a relapse, very simply tell the adolescents that you want them to plan their next relapse and share that with the group. In order to do this, I have them write out the answers to the following questions:

■ Tell us how your relapse will begin.

■ Tell us what you will do two weeks before, one week before, three days before, and the day of your relapse.

■ Tell us who you will blame, what decisions you will make, what resentments you will hold, what you will feel sorry for yourself about, and how you will con yourself.

In many ways, this relapse prevention technique is a paradox which utilizes prescribing the symptoms. It is very powerful because it requires that adolescents be excruciatingly honest with themselves and think at length about how they will set up their failure. It also gives adolescents the very powerful message that they have the means to prevent the relapse if they choose to utilize the recovery skills. It is also helpful to refer them back to their self-described relapse process when they begin displaying relapse symptoms.

3. Recognizing the Return to Denial: It is important to teach adolescents how to recognize the return of their "stinking thinking." This is done by asking the adolescents what types of situations usually trigger denial thoughts (i.e., what are the emotional, social or psychological dimensions of this denial), and what kind of thinking usually kicks off the denial process (i.e., what do you tell yourself to make it okay to use). Once adolescents have identified these situations and thoughts, I ask them to monitor these on a daily basis and share them with me or the group. I teach the adolescents that these thoughts lose their power when verbalized and shared with others. I also point out to adolescents that they need to learn that thinking those thoughts are a serious danger sign for them. They need to learn to discipline themselves not to believe their own denial. I have even had adolescents write down their denial on a piece of paper, and draw a phrase and symbol (i.e., skull and cross bones) on top of it to signify that those thoughts are poison for them.

Insure that the relapsed adolescents remain appropriate participants in the treatment process.

Relapsed adolescents should not be given any special status if they are being treated in a group setting. This special status often comes from their knowledge and that makes it very easy for staff and facilitators to rely on them to confront and educate the other adolescents. Giving special status to these adolescents can be avoided by some very simple but respectful interventions directed at the relapsed individual. For example, when another member of the group begins talking about the fact that they feel their use is not a problem, it is very common for the relapsed adolescent to begin confronting this individual on the errors in his thinking. The facilitator can intervene in this interaction by asking the relapsed adolescent to identify how very similar thinking contributed to his relapse and also to identify examples of how he continues to think in such a fashion. If at all possible, it is helpful for relapsed adolescents to be in group with at least one other relapsed adolescent. They are much less likely to allow one another to slip through with pat answers and compliance. It is also helpful if relapsed adolescents work with a more experienced counselor. It has been my experience that most kids with any time in the program have a tremendous amount of program knowledge. New counselors, in particular, can often be intimidated by this situation, leaving the door open for manipulation on the part of the adolescent.

ADDRESSING OTHER
RELEVANT CLINICAL ISSUES.

My research examining clinical issues for teens who have relapsed clearly identifies for us that adolescents who relapse are adolescents who have experienced significant loss or trauma, have emotional or behavioral problems in addition to their addiction, and have alcoholic parents. It is clinically irresponsible to ignore these issues for relapsed adolescents. It is the professional's job to work with the adolescent to determine the extent to which these other issues contributed to the relapse and to spend some significant time fairly early in the recovery process addressing and moving toward resolution of these issues.

As outlined in this chapter, professionals can be very effective in motivating relapsed kids to re-enter recovery and in assisting them in stabilizing and maintaining a recovery process. Perhaps the most important characteristic for counselors who work with relapsed kids is the counselor's ability to continue to believe in the adolescents and have faith in their ability to make the changes they need to make in order to succeed.

**Relapsed adolescents need
relapse-specific
treatment assignments.**

If the relapsed adolescent has had a previous treatment experience, he does not need to repeat all the tasks of the first experience. When they are asked to complete the same first step in the same drug history, they quickly begin to coast. These treatment assignments need to be specifically connected to the relapse process. If they were able to achieve abstinence for any period of time following their first treatment experience, it is safe to assume that they have some basic knowledge and recovery skills. It is more helpful to focus on a relapse drug history and a relapse first step which is designed to assist the adolescent in developing a true understanding of their personal relapse dynamic. In order to understand this dynamic, adolescents need to focus on what behaviors, attitudes, and thoughts led to relapse. They must focus on how they convinced themselves it was okay to return to use, what they did to attempt to control their use and how this failed. They then need to trace the progression of their relapse and give specific examples of this progression. Finally, they need to compare the extent and consequences of their use during the relapse to the extent and consequences prior to their first recovery attempt.

CHAPTER
12
THE DEVELOPMENTAL MODEL
OF FAMILY RECOVERY

I was once a participant in a workshop in which we were discussing family therapy issues. One of the participants shook her head, sighed and stated, "Families, there must be a better way." This comment reflects the frustration that many professionals experience in attempting to engage the family of the adolescent in the recovery process. Studies conducted by CATOR (1987) indicate that family involvement in the treatment and early recovery for adolescents is a critical indicator of success. Professionals who treat families of addicted teens struggle with the same dilemma as individuals who treat the teens. Much of the traditional wisdom of addiction family programming and literature is designed for family members of adult patients. As a result, many counselors struggle with determining the appropriate and effective family treatment direction for parents. Parents complain that ALANON appears to be more geared toward spouses than parents. Parents often indicate that they feel their needs cannot be met by these meetings. Family recovery is critical and family programming must be modified so that it is respectful and appropriate for parents. This chapter discusses family recovery and relapse prevention. Before undertaking this discussion, however, it is important to examine a much more basic issue—the issue of the counselor's attitude toward the parents with whom they are working.

AN ISSUE OF RESPECT

When conducting training for professionals who work with adolescents, I often ask them to make a list of descriptive words which they use when discussing parents served by their agency, facility, or treatment center. This list includes a long litany of negative and hostile adjectives and statements. After reading the list, I ask counselors how they would feel as a parent coming to that particular facility or agency for help or assistance, given how parents are viewed. Counselors often respond that they would be somewhat reluctant and even resistant to the process. My point is very simple. Much of what is labeled as resistance on the part of the parent has its roots in the parent's guilt about what has happened to their child and their fear that they will be labeled, judged, and criticized. Regardless of how nice, concerned, or cooperative counselors attempt to be toward parents, if the prevailing attitude toward parents is negative, parents will be resistant to participating. Many adolescent counselors, myself included, elected to work with adolescents initially because we could relate to them and empathize with them. Much of this empathy stems from our own unresolved issues with our family of origin. However, it quickly became apparent to me that in order to provide any effective level of care for adolescents, I needed to shift my view of myself from that of an adolescent advocate to one of a family advocate.

Disrespectful attitudes toward families are evident not only in how professionals feel about and describe parents, but also in how we develop and design program services for the family members of the adolescents. For years, addiction professionals insisted on conducting family week meetings Monday through Friday. Parents of addicted and dual diagnosed teens have often missed a tremendous amount of work in order to attend school conferences, court dates, meetings with probation officers, and trips to the doctor. As a result, many of them are unable to take another three to five days off to participate in a family week program. Most professionals have come to recognize that although the family week format works well for the treatment program and has some strong therapeutic value, it is impractical for working parents. If we view ourselves as advocates for the parents as well as the adolescents, it is important to make therapy and treatment accessible to the parents. This includes evening and weekend programming. Making programming accessible to family members is very simply an issue of respect. Similarly, providing programming that is specifically designed to meet parents' needs is an issue of respect. Respect is a critical factor and is also an assumption which underlies the content put forth in the rest of this chapter.

FAMILY PRETREATMENT

Tammy Bell has done a great deal to advance the concept of pretreatment in working with addicted teens (Bell, 1990). Bell describes pretreatment as "the last phase of active use and the first phase of recovery". Very simply stated, pretreatment recognizes that recovery is a process and respects the fact that getting ready to get clean and sober is a very critical piece of the process. Pretreatment works with adolescents who are not motivated to change by helping them to recognize that as long as they continue to use mood-altering chemicals, there will be unpleasant consequences.

The concept of family pretreatment builds on Bell's theory and recognizes that change and recovery for parents is a developmental process much as it is for adolescents. In this process, families are faced with a series of tasks which they must accomplish during their journey toward health and healing. This model examines the tasks which families face at each point in the recovery process and recognizes that families must complete these tasks before moving to the next phase. It is the job of the professional to assess accurately where the family is in the process of recovery and to develop treatment strategies designed to help them continue to move forward. The social work expression "start where your client is" is particularly applicable here. When parents do not join in the process of change, it is time for the counselor to consider that perhaps the family has not completed pretreatment tasks and the counselor has moved ahead of the family in the process.

Upon initial contact with counselors, therapists, and treatment centers, many parents have not recovered from the initial shock they experienced upon being told that their child's use of chemicals or behavior is a problem. In order for parents to participate willingly in the process of change, they must first recognize and accept that there is a reason for them to approach things differently. Recognizing and accepting the need for change is a process that often takes time. Families that are motivated for change have completed their pretreatment tasks.

Some parents are able to accomplish this process independently and some have done so with the help of professionals. It is useless to proceed with tasks designed to bring about change until parents have come to the realization that change is necessary. Recognizing that change is necessary is the work of pre treatment for parents and includes the following:

■ Parents accept the truth about their child's use of mood-altering chemicals, behavior and/or psychiatric diagnosis and the implications of this use, behavior, and diagnosis.

■ Parents recognize that a problem exists that is beyond their control.

■ Parents recognize that continuing to address this problem the way they have previously addressed it will not bring about the change which they desire.

■ Parents develop a trusting relationship with a helping professional.

EARLY RECOVERY

Once the parents have completed the pretreatment process, they will be ready to tackle the tasks of early recovery.

These tasks include:

■ Parents become willing to assume parental responsibility in the family.

■ Parents do not tolerate inappropriate behavior on the part of their child.

■ Parents recognize their own behavior which contributes to or enables the adolescent's use of chemicals or other behavioral problems.

■ Parents become willing to work with others to develop healthy family living skills which include improved communication, effective parenting, family problem-solving and information about the issue or disorder which their child is addressing.

■ Families become more open-minded in considering the need for developing an ongoing recovery program for themselves.

During early recovery, the parents have been empowered to resume a healthy control over their family and shift the power from the adolescent to the parent, where it rightfully belongs. By accomplishing the tasks of early recovery, chaos has been reduced and structure has been restored to the family system. These tasks are critical because once the family has completed pretreatment tasks and recognizes and accepts the truth about the child's behavior, it is understandable that their early recovery focus is on addressing this behavior. It is the professional's job to assist the family in addressing and learning to manage in a healthy fashion their chemically dependent or dually diagnosed adolescent. When parents feel they have regained control of the home, the family is ready to move to the next level of recovery. In this next phase, parents begin to shift the focus from the adolescent's behavior to themselves.

MIDDLE RECOVERY

Families are now ready for the middle stage of recovery. The family tasks in middle-stage recovery include the following:

■ Parents realize that they must make decisions regarding their life and their recovery that are independent of their child's recovery. Parents must decide they will live full, healthy and sane lives regardless of what their children decide to do with their own recovery program.

■ Parents assume responsibility for opening up their world and developing a rewarding lifestyle that expands beyond their role as parents to their addicted or dually diagnosed child.

■ Parents realize that in order to accomplish tasks one and two, they need to assume complete and total responsibility for their behavior, feelings, and attitudes.

■ Parents become willing to explore issues beyond their child's use of chemicals and psychiatric diagnosis which will prevent them from achieving their goal of developing a happy and rewarding life.

These issues may include marital problems, the parents' own use of alcohol or mood-altering chemicals, family of origin issues, destructive behavior cycles, or compulsive behavior.

It has been my experience that most families do not complete phase three for approximately six months. I once conducted the family program for an adolescent intensive outpatient program. The program was designed to allow families to participate three hours per week for six months. At the end of that six months, 75% or more of the family members sought a referral for help in dealing with their own lifestyle problems. While a handful of families were ready for these referrals prior to the six-month period, what became very obvious to me was that the change for parents is a process and that this process takes time. If we expect parents to reach this stage of recovery, we must be respectful and aware of the fact that there is very little substitute for time in the process of change and healing.

Middle-stage recovery for families is an awareness and decision making phase. Once these tasks have been accomplished, the parents are ready to move forward to the advanced recovery phase.

ADVANCED RECOVERY

Advanced recovery tasks include the following:

- Parents continue to increase their supports and enhance their lives beyond their addicted or dually diagnosed child.

- Parents begin the process of addressing and resolving their own lifestyle issues.

It is impossible to put a time frame on this phase of recovery. Resolution of lifestyle issues is a very individual process and is in itself an ongoing process for parents. Entrance into this phase does create a dramatic shift in family dynamics because it represents a major movement toward health for the parents. As parents move toward resolution of lifestyle issues and changes, they move toward a maintenance phase of recovery.

MAINTENANCE

The tasks of maintenance include the following:

- Parents continue to respond to the parenting challenges presented by their addicted adolescent as well as the other children in the home.

- Parents are able to maintain the structure within the family system and respond appropriately to the relapse and/or recovery issues presented by the addicted child.

- Parents maintain healthy lifestyle changes which they have worked to develop.

- Parents are able to assist the family in successfully negotiating any developmental challenges or crises which the family faces.

- Families seek appropriate assistance when they begin to feel "stuck" in regard to family issues.

- Family members continue to take responsibility for addressing and resolving lifestyle issues.

The focus of this chapter will be on facilitating the parents' completion of the pretreatment tasks of recovery and early and middle recovery (i.e., relapse prevention). For more information regarding early and middle recovery tasks, readers can refer to the author's first book, A Professional's Guide to Dual Disorders in Adolescents (Gabe, 1989).

FAMILY PRETREATMENT: MOTIVATING FAMILIES FOR CHANGE

The task of the therapist during family pretreatment is to assist the family in accepting the truth about their child's behavior, drug use, or psychiatric condition and to elicit parental support for the adolescent's treatment process. In order for pretreatment tasks to be accomplished, the therapist and the family must develop a partnership. If the parents are not in support of the treatment recommendations being made for their child, the family will unintentionally sabotage the child's treatment or will allow the child to manipulate the experience. Counselors often make the mistake of moving forward with a treatment direction without the full support and cooperation of the family. Just as it sometimes takes adolescents a while to recognize the need for change, it also often takes families a while to recognize this need. In most cases, attempting to force a treatment recommendation on the family when the family is not ready to accept that recommendation results in an unproductive power struggle.

All treatment of adolescents begins with an accurate assessment of the adolescent and the adolescent's family. For more information regarding the comprehensive assessment process, refer to the author's first book (Gabe, 1989). The assessment process is often the first step of pretreatment for family members. A great deal of valuable pretreatment work can be done during the assessment. It is important that the professional remember that the assessment provides a valuable opportunity to begin to engage the family in the process of change. The therapist must make sure to take time to begin to develop a relationship with the family. Following are techniques which will assist in engaging the family in the process:

- Recognize that most family members are nervous, uncomfortable, and guilt-ridden. The professional must do everything possible early in the session to help put the family at ease, to assist them in developing a feeling that they are being supported and to assure them that they are not being judged. It is often wise to take time to listen to family members before asking questions and filling out forms. The questions and forms are sometimes intimidating and frightening to parents.

■ Pick up on words or phrases that family members use to describe the problem and emphasize these phrases when talking with them. Parents may indicate they are concerned about their child's use and they may even indicate that they feel their child uses too much. However, this is very different from parents saying that their child is addicted. If a parent indicates that they feel their child has a drug problem and the counselor asks the parent how long they felt the child has been addicted, it is not unusual for parents to become defensive and point out that they did not say that their child was addicted. Therefore, if a parent says that they are worried that their child is using too often, the counselor needs to ask questions such as, "When did you begin to be concerned that your child was using too often?" Parents are often similarly resistant to psychiatric terms such as depression.

■ Be respectful of family members by using words they understand, avoiding labels and professional jargon or terminology.

■ Stay focused on the adolescent's problem. When professionals shift the focus from the child's presenting problem to issues such as marital problems or parental drinking, family members become defensive and very often do not come back for a second session.

■ Attempt to elevate the parents' status in the family by complimenting the family on strengths that you recognize. I often find myself applauding parents for their courage to make an appointment and the effort they put forth to keep the appointment.

■ Let the parents know that you are aware that they have tried to solve this problem and invite them to share what has worked well and what has not worked. Very simply asking the parents what they have done to try to address this problem communicates to the parents that you know they have been actively seeking a solution. It also lays the ground work for pretreatment as it helps the parents recognize that their efforts to solve the problem on their own have not been successful.

Once the counselor has worked to begin to develop a relationship with the parents, the next step is to empower the parents through the assessment process. Upon completion of a comprehensive assessment, professionals make recommendations regarding their opinion of the appropriate level of care for the adolescent. If done correctly, this process can facilitate the completion of pretreatment for parents by empowering parents to take control and assert themselves as competent heads of their household.

Out of respect for parents and in order to further engage the parents in the process of change, I suggest that professionals meet with the parents without the adolescent present and present their recommendations for the prescriptive course of treatment for the adolescent and the reasons for these recommendations. If the parents accept the recommendations for treatment, the counselor spends some time preparing the parents to present the recommendations to the adolescent. It is important for the professional to make sure that both parents are supportive of the recommendations and that they will voice to the adolescent what they want the adolescent to do. It is very tempting for the professional to present the recommendation to the adolescent and "play the bad guy." It is important to keep in mind that it is the parents' job to establish behavioral expectations for the child and to set limits. By presenting their stance on the adolescent's course of treatment to the adolescent, the parents are assuming their appropriate role.

I often find it helpful to prepare the parents for this confrontation with their child by asking them what their child does when he or she is trying to manipulate them. Parents can usually quickly tell me that the children make threats, cry, get angry, etc. We then problem-solve appropriate ways for the parents to respond should the adolescent display this behavior. In addition, I often share with them other reactions that adolescents display in an attempt to manipulate their parents. Once I am comfortable that the parents are prepared for this discussion with the adolescent, I ask the adolescent to join us. I encourage and support the parents in presenting the plans for treatment to the adolescent. Almost without exception, adolescents immediately launch into the various techniques they use to get control in the family. Family members, with a little coaching, respond to this in a very competent and appropriate fashion. This very simple task accomplishes several important dynamic changes within the system.

- Parents very quickly become committed to following through with the treatment recommendation. Parents who are committed are much more likely to follow through, much less likely to be manipulated, and more likely to be cooperative.

- It elevates the parents' position in the family and gives the clear message to everyone that in order for the family to change, the parents must be part of the process.

- It shifts the power dynamics from the adolescent back to the parent. Power in the family needs to belong to the parent. It is important to re-establish that hierarchy early in the treatment process.

- It increases the parents' sense of competence in their parenting ability. As the adolescent attempts to manipulate the parents and the parents respond appropriately, it is easy to see their level of confidence in themselves increase.

- It provides a very clear message to everyone that the parents, not the therapist, are in charge of the family.

If the assessment is conducted appropriately, the process of change has already begun to happen even before formal treatment begins.

If parents are not willing to support the counselor's recommendations, it is important for the counselor to negotiate to determine precisely what the parents are willing to do. Parents, because of their own denial, often feel that others are overreacting to the situation or that the recommended level of intervention is premature or too severe. For example, it is not unusual for parents to tell me that AA is not necessary for the child and that outpatient counseling will be adequate. If parents do not support a recommendation for twelve step attendance, it is unlikely that the child will attend the meetings. I caution professionals not to bypass families and push recommendations that make families uncomfortable. The end result will be that the parents will sabotage further attempts to work with the child. When the parents are unwilling to follow through with the treatment recommendations, professionals must continue to work with families from a pretreatment mode.

I usually begin my pretreatment work with family members by presenting my recommendations and my reasons for them. If the family members are hesitant or resistant to these recommendations, I invite an open discussion about their resistance or hesitation. I let parents know that ultimately, the decision as to what course of treatment their child will follow is up to them. (The exception to this is when I am treating a suicidal adolescent or an adolescent whose use is so severe that the child is in immediate danger if he/she is not hospitalized.) Various levels of intervention are described and discussed. After this discussion, I ask the parents what level of intervention they could comfortably accept. I generally try to negotiate a level of treatment which will allow me to continue to work with the adolescent and the family in a group or individual setting at least one time per week. Once we have determined an appropriate course of treatment, I continue in the manner described earlier in which I encourage the parents to present this to the adolescent.

It is important to understand that resistance to appropriate treatment recommendations stems from parental denial, the parents' belief that they will be able to handle the problem on their own, and lack of appropriate information. When this happens, it is the task of the professional to move the parents gently toward a more realistic view of their child's situation. In order to do this, I make predictions regarding what I think will happen with their child. I might say to a family: "I know that you believe that this course of action is most appropriate for your child. I hope it works and that we see some significant improvement. However, it has been my experience that when an adolescent experiences this degree of difficulty, a more intensive level of care is required."

I then move into a more active phase of negotiating with the family. I say to the family, "I know it's important to you that things get better. It is also important that we examine what changes we expect to happen here. Can you tell me what you expect to see, what kinds of things will help you to know that things are getting better with your child?" Once we have established this, I ask the family, "If things do not get better, what will that mean to you?" At this point, I am trying to help the parents move through their denial by recognizing that after all this, if the child's behavior does not improve, the problem is indeed more serious than they are willing to accept. I then ask my final pretreatment question of the family: "If this does not work, and your child's problem behavior or use continues, what will you be willing to do?" Even the most resistant family members often acknowledge that if they are unable to handle the problem on their own or if this level of intervention does not work, they will need to consider the possibility that their child's use or behavior is worse than they initially thought and that they may need to follow a recommendation for a more intensive or restrictive level of care.

I then try to establish my partnership with the parents further by stating to them, "It's very important that we stay in close communication. I think we should evaluate the situation in another six weeks to see if we're on the right track. If there's another crisis before that time or if things don't improve or if things get worse, we'll talk about what we need to do next." Almost without exception, my predictions about the child's behavior come true and within a very short period of time, the parents come to me and acknowledge that the situation is worse than they initially believed and they recognize the need to do something different.

It is important to remember that this format can be used to overcome resistance to almost any treatment recommendation. For example, the family may be resisting the need for family therapy, AA attendance by their child, or ALANON attendance by themselves.

This resistance decreases as families prove to themselves that "their way" is not resulting in the desired changes.

CHAPTER

13

UNDERSTANDING FAMILY SYSTEM RELAPSE

Professionals who work with parents of addicted and dually diagnosed adolescents often encourage those parents to focus on their own recovery more and focus less on their child's recovery; however, we do very little to educate parents about the symptoms of family system relapse. While it is important to provide parents with an overview of relapse dynamics in adolescents, it is just as important to provide them with information regarding family system relapse. I once received a call from an aftercare family with whom I was working. They requested a family session and when I asked the nature of the concern, they indicated that they had relapsed. When I inquired about their child's use, they informed me that the child had not used drugs, but the family had lapsed into old behaviors, and they wanted to intervene before it got completely out of hand. This is an example of a family truly in recovery.

The remainder of this chapter discusses parental relapse and the signs and symptoms that we utilize when we work with families.

1. **PARENTS ARE NOT ABLE TO MOVE THE FOCUS FROM THE CHEMICALLY DEPENDENT CHILD TO EVALUATE THE FAMILY SYSTEM.**

As the adolescent's use of chemicals and behaviors become more and more problematic, the family finds itself focusing on the addicted adolescent. Maintaining the focus on the addicted or problem adolescent often serves an important purpose in the family. It provides family members with a common cause and it provides parents with a focus that allows them to ignore the other issues in the family.

Early recovery requires that family members begin to look at the family as an interactive system in which all members must continue to evaluate their own attitudes and behaviors. When this evaluation becomes difficult or threatening, it is easier for family members to resume their focus on the adolescent. This is frustrating for adolescents, particularly adolescents early in recovery when parents and other family members continue to treat them as though they are using, even when they are not. This particular relapse dynamic demonstrates how family systems some times need the drug addicted or psychiatrically impaired member in order for them to maintain their comfortable status quo.

2. FAMILY MEMBERS OVERREACT TO THE ADOLESCENT'S BEHAVIOR.

Parents who have spent a significant amount of time worried about their adolescent's use often find themselves overreacting to normal adolescent behavior even after the adolescent's use has been discontinued. It is not unusual for parents to spend a great deal of time in parent groups complaining about the adolescent talking too much on the phone, making irresponsible decisions, and other normal adolescent infractions of the rules. Family members often react to this normal adolescent limit-testing with the same intensity that they reacted to their adolescent's use, suspensions from school, and arrest. When dealing with an addicted adolescent, families often develop a tolerance for high-level chaos and conflict. It is easy to relapse into this pattern of conflict even when the situation does not warrant it.

3. PARENTS USE PROGRAM CONCEPTS SUCH AS DETACHMENT TO AVOID PARENTAL RESPONSIBILITY.

Parents of addicted kids often feel exhausted and battle fatigued. Prior to the adolescent's coming to treatment, many parents feel they have battled the child's behavior to no avail. Many of them are exhausted, feeling incompetent to parent their children, and would love to have a break from parenting. There is a great deal of confusion about how one detaches while still remaining a responsible parent. As a result of this confusion, parents often interpret detachment as abdicating parental control and abandoning parental responsibility.

Early in my work with addicted adolescents, I attended a multi-agency staffing for a fourteen-year-old and her family. A member of one of the agencies asked the girl's mother what types of rules and limits had been established for the adolescent in the home. The mother informed the group that she was practicing the concept of detachment which she had learned in my parent group. She said that she learned in parent group that she could not control her child and, therefore, was not attempting to set any limits on her. Imagine my horrified reaction as all eyes turned to me astounded that I would counsel a parent to abdicate parental responsibility. Although we talk extensively in our parent group about parenting skills and appropriate use of consequences, when parents become frustrated they often forget the discussions on parenting and remember other pieces of the program. This was the case in this example. When parents are confused or overwhelmed by the early recovery tasks that face them, it is not unusual for them to select bits and pieces of the program to use as a rationalization for not continuing with the difficult task of learning how to parent an addicted or dually diagnosed adolescent.

4. **FAMILY MEMBERS CEASE TO WORK THEIR OWN RECOVERY PROGRAMS (I.E., FAMILY MEMBERS DO NOT ASSUME RESPONSIBILITY FOR THEIR BEHAVIOR, DECISIONS, AND CHOICES.)**

Recovery is first and foremost about assuming responsibility for oneself. During times of stress, it is very easy for parents to become frustrated and blame other people (particularly the adolescent) for their own behavior, feelings, decisions, and choices. During early recovery, we attempt to stress to parents that they are totally responsible for how they react to their child's behavior and their child's use. Parents find it very easy to blame their children for how they themselves are reacting to the children.

I worked with a family who was so focused on their adolescent's behavior that they ceased to have a life of their own. The parents enjoyed square dancing, but had not square danced for several years because they felt they needed to be home on Friday night to deal with whatever crisis might surface. During early recovery the parents often talked about wanting to resume their Friday night square dancing but chose not to do so because they felt they had to stay home in case another crisis surfaced. Several months went by without a typical Friday night crisis but the parents continued to stay at home and worry and anticipate that a crisis was inevitable. They then blamed the recovering adolescent for the fact that they could not participate in their square dancing. These parents were not assuming responsibility for their decision about Friday nights and unfairly blamed their adolescent for a decision that was theirs to make.

5. **THE FAMILY REMAINS A CLOSED SYSTEM THAT DOES NOT OPEN ITSELF UP TO CORRECTIVE FEEDBACK.**

High-risk families in general and families with addiction problems tend to erect barriers between themselves and the outside world. The more the addiction progresses, the more closed the family system becomes to feedback. As the system closes itself off, members in the system begin to lose their ability to perceive accurately what is happening in their family. During the course of active addiction (regardless of whether we are talking about a parental addiction or an adolescent addiction), the family becomes more and more cut off from support such as church, friends, and extended family. Early recovery provides an opportunity to open the system. During family system relapse times, the system again begins to close itself off and repeat its unhealthy patterns of behavior.

6. **FAMILY MEMBERS BLAME ONE ANOTHER FOR THEIR PROBLEMS.**

During active addiction, family members often blame others for their behavior while assuming responsibility for the behavior of others. For example, parents often blame themselves, one another, peers, schools, and communities for their child's use instead of holding the child responsible. Similarly, parents may blame the adolescent for the parents' own loss of control. I have frequently known parents who blamed their children for pushing them into becoming physically aggressive with their children. During early recovery, members of the family are encouraged to assume responsibility for themselves and to allow others to do the same. As families move into a relapse mode, they resume the stance of blaming others. Very common relapse behavior during early recovery stems from parents not being able to agree on how to parent their teenager. When parents argue about how to parent their child, they end up in conflict with one another and often blame the child for this.

7. PARENTS TREAT THE ADOLESCENT AS IF HE/SHE IS STILL USING.

Parents are often unaware that they are continuing to react to their child as if he/she is using when there is no indication of use. For example, parents may continue to monitor their children's phone calls, randomly search their room, or even follow the adolescent to school although there is absolutely no reason to continue this behavior. As addiction progresses within a family, parents often ignore family business to focus on the addiction and/or addiction-related behavior. Once the adolescent discontinues their use, parents often find themselves faced with many unresolved issues. These issues include the parents' relationship with one another, their relationship with their other children, their relationship with extended family and often their relationship with friends and co-workers. It becomes painful and difficult to address these issues and parents may respond to this by shifting their focus back to the adolescent and returning to policing behavior which allows them to continue to ignore other family business.

8. FAMILY MEMBERS SABOTAGE ONE ANOTHER'S RECOVERY.

This sabotage takes place in many different ways. One of the most common sabotage behaviors stems from resentments toward family members' participation in self-help meetings. If one parent decides to become very active in ALANON and one parent does not, resentments often build. Similarly, parents may be highly resentful of or uncomfortable about their child's involvement in AA or NA. The parents may become judgmental about other individuals in the program and make statements such as, "I don't want my child associating with all those drunks," or "I don't want my wife hanging around with all those nut cases in ALANON." It is not unusual that parents unwittingly sabotage their adolescents by not assisting them in getting transportation to the meetings, not allowing the adolescents to attend meetings during the week, telling the adolescents they must be home at 9:00 p.m. when the meetings do not adjourn until 9:00 p.m., and complaining that the adolescents are using the meetings to socialize. Similarly, the parents may even ground adolescents and not let them attend meetings while they are grounded. I once had a parent call me complaining that she wanted to put an end to the meeting "nonsense" because she felt her child was having too good a time through his involvement in the self-help program.

9. PARENTS ENGAGE IN CONFLICT WITH THEIR CHILD'S COUNSELOR, SPONSOR, OR PROGRAM FRIENDS.

During the adolescent's active use, parents have often tried many things to intervene in their child's drinking or drug use. Parents often become frustrated or hurt when they feel that their child would not listen to them, yet he/she is responding to a "total stranger." Parents often feel confused about why their child is so willing to talk to an adult sponsor, but so reluctant to talk to them. When these feelings are not discussed and dealt with, it is easy for parents to take a conflictual stance with the child's sponsor or counselor. This conflict often becomes intensified because the more the parent disapproves of the sponsor, the more important the sponsor becomes to the child.

10. UNHEALTHY AND INAPPROPRIATE INTERACTIONS OCCUR BETWEEN PARENTS AND THEIR CHILDREN.

If a parent is recovering from an addiction, that parent may be tempted to become over-involved in the adolescent's program. Often when an adult in the family is recovering from their own addiction, they have many regrets about the time they lost and the opportunities they missed to develop a relationship with their child. When parents enter into recovery from their addiction, they often find themselves isolated from their children and do not know how to go about rebuilding that relationship. When the child enters into recovery from addiction, the recovering parent often feels they finally have a common bond. As a result, the parent attempts to act as the child's sponsor instead of their parent. I can recall several family sessions in which the recovering addicted parent and the recovering addicted adolescent would sit in family therapy and exchange program slogans as they did not know what else to say to one another.

In some family systems, the recovering adolescent becomes the most functional person within that system. In such systems, it is very easy for the child to become parentified. Parents may inappropriately confide in their child as if their child were a friend or partner. Parents may ask the recovering child to "talk to" a younger sibling about the sibling's use. Similarly, a non-using parent may ask the recovering child to talk to the addicted parent about their use. One common example of parentification is parents sharing with their children concerns or problems they have with one another.

Parents triangulate children, professional helpers, and extended family members. Early in the recovery process, communicating directly with family members can become extremely stressful. In order to reduce or alleviate stress, the family members often bring a third member into the dyad, thereby creating a triangle. For example, if parents have a difficult time communicating directly with one another, they may communicate through their children or through members of the extended family. When parents do not want to address their adolescent's acting out behavior directly, they triangulize helpers by fighting with their spouses about their adolescent's behavior and then asking the counselor to intervene for them. The triangles take many shapes and can include a variety of different relationships. Triangles serve as a way to avoid direct communication with other members of the family.

11. IF THESE PRECEDING RELAPSE WARNING SIGNS ARE NOT ADDRESSED AND RESOLVED, ONE OF THE FOLLOWING IS LIKELY TO HAPPEN:

■ The addicted person will sense the stress and conflict in the family and will relapse in order to provide the family with a focus and reduce the family anxiety.

■ Unresolved conflicts will surface between parents and this provides a tremendous threat to the system. If the addicted adolescent does not relapse, another member of the family will attempt to relieve the family's anxiety by becoming emotionally, behaviorally, or physically symptomatic.

■ Relationships will deteriorate to the point that parents may separate or even divorce.

■ Parents will recognize the crisis of the relapse and will decide to address and resolve these relapse behaviors as part of the recovery process.

Understanding this family relapse dynamic is the critical first step to preventing family relapse and promote family recovery. Family relapse prevention and interventions are discussed in the next chapter.

Chapter

14

FAMILY RELAPSE PREVENTION

There are several simple and specific family treatment interventions which can be utilized in the early recovery process to prevent or counteract family system relapse.

1. **ASSIST THE FAMILY IN SHIFTING THE FOCUS FROM THE ADOLESCENT IN ORDER TO EVALUATE AND ACCEPT THE FAMILY AS A SYSTEM.**

   This can be accomplished in early recovery by simply asking the family members how they feel and how they react to various behaviors displayed by the addicted adolescent. It is helpful to include parents as well as siblings in this process. As parents and siblings begin to share their feelings and examine their behavior, they begin to accept the family as an interactive network. It is also helpful to ask families to evaluate the effectiveness of their responses to the addicted adolescent. This can be done by asking very simple questions such as, "How do you react when your child comes home under the influence?" "What are you trying to accomplish with this reaction?" "How well did this reaction work?"

2. **ATTEMPT TO NARROW THE FOCUS OF THE FAMILY'S CONCERN TO PREVENT OVERREACTION TO THE ADDICTED TEEN OR TO NORMAL ADOLESCENT BEHAVIOR.**

   I often ask family members to list all of the behaviors and problems demonstrated by their adolescent which concern them. Once this task is accomplished, I ask them to prioritize these concerns, listing their biggest concern first and their least significant concern last. Once they have accomplished this, I often review their list and critique it. This provides an opportunity to help reframe the parents' view of the behavior as well as to provide them with education about what is normal adolescent behavior versus what is pathological behavior. In reviewing the list I often indicate to them, "This is normal adolescent behavior and is to be expected. Although as parents you'll have to deal with it, it doesn't indicate a drug use or other problems on the part of the adolescent." I then point out to the parents that in the next few months we will focus our energy on addressing the top five concerns on the list. We then discuss appropriate and effective parental responses to these top five behaviors. This approach assists the family members or parents in not over reacting to insignificant but annoying behavior on the part of the adolescent. It contributes to reducing chaos and creating an atmosphere of calm and manageability within the system.

3. DURING EARLY FAMILY RECOVERY, IT IS IMPORTANT TO FOCUS ON RESPONSIBLE PARENTING.

When discussing the recovery concept of detachment with parents, it is important to point out that detachment means that parents are responsible for reclaiming control over their emotions, their behavior and their reactions to the adolescent. Detachment does not mean abdicating parental responsibility. I consistently and gently remind parents that it is their job to parent their addicted child and that their addicted child will need a great deal of parenting in order to remain chemically free and develop into a responsible young adult.

4. FOCUS ON INDIVIDUAL RESPONSIBILITY.

I find myself gently reminding parents early in recovery that everyone in the family is responsible for his own behavior. Parents often complain that they argue with one another because they cannot agree on how to parent their child. This creates conflict in the relationship and they blame this conflict on the adolescent. It is important for parents that they know they are the parents and that it is their job to learn how to work together to parent their child.

If they disagree, and this disagreement creates conflict then it is a problem that belongs to them and not their child.

In order to assist the family in sorting out problem ownership, I often use a very simple art therapy technique. I ask each member of the family to take a sheet of paper and draw a T- shirt. I then ask them to write their name on the T-shirt because that shirt belongs to them. I then review the list of family problems which they have identified and tell them that it is our job to sort out who owns each problem, behavior, and feeling. We then work to put everyone's problems, feelings, and behaviors on their T-shirt. For example, I might say to Dad: "Dad, you own your temper and your anger. You need to write those two things on your T-shirt. It doesn't matter what other people in the family do that makes you angry, this anger is yours. You need to learn to deal with it." "Mom, you give in too easily when your child begs or badgers you and you need to put that on your T-shirt." "Susy, you need to abide by your curfew and go to school. These are your issues and the belong on your T-shirt." Once the T-shirt activity has been initiated, it is helpful to return to it at different times during the early recovery process when new issues surface and old issues resurface and ask the family to stop and decide on whose T-shirt these issues belong.

I once had a young person come into my office and tell me that his family had a particularly difficult week. He indicated that his father had become very angry and in the process of being angry had become verbally abusive to the adolescent. The adolescent stated that previously when his father became angry and yelled at him, the adolescent would end up blaming himself for his father's behavior and telling himself what a loser he was. He stated that this time he reminded himself that his father's temper was his father's problem and just because his father was losing his temper it did not mean that he was a bad kid. He also informed me that his father became even further enraged when he apologized to his father for his behavior and reminded him that his temper belonged on his T-shirt. The father joined me in the session later and was very annoyed when he reported to me what his son had done. He stated,

"He told me that my anger belonged on my T-shirt. Can you believe that?" I responded to the father that it seemed to me that his son was very accurate. The Dad responded, "I know. That's what made me so mad."

5. GIVE ASSIGNMENTS DESIGNED TO OPEN UP THE FAMILY SYSTEM.

The more open the system remains, the less likely it is to relapse into unproductive and unhealthy behavior. Family attendance at the family group, parental attendance at ALANON, and the adolescent's attendance at self-help groups are opportunities for opening up a family system. In addition, the therapist might want to work with families to explore other opportunities to open the system. I often encourage parents to resume contact with friends they have not seen for a while, reconnect with extended family members, and pursue activities that they previously enjoyed. The more open the system, the more objective family members can be in evaluating and reviewing the activities of that system. This also encourages the parents to develop a lifestyle that is more balanced and less child-focused.

6. ESTABLISHING GUIDELINES FOR HEALTHY AND APPROPRIATE COMMUNICATION AND INTERACTION.

Families often need help in restoring structure and boundaries within the system. I often talk with parents about guide lines for appropriate interaction boundaries. In this discussion, I give them very specific guidelines as to subjects that are not appropriate to discuss with their child. This listing includes items such as: "It is not appropriate for you as a parent to discuss your conflicts with one another with your adolescent. It is not appropriate to ask adolescents to parent your other children. It is not appropriate to disagree about household rules or consequences in front of your child." When an adolescent becomes parentified in the system, it is helpful to point this out to the parents. I find myself saying, "Mom, Susy's trying to be the Mom in this family and I think we both agree that that's your job. I am going to talk to Susy and ask her not to do that and I'd like you to discuss this with her as well."

7. DO NOT GET HOOKED INTO DOING THINGS FOR PARENTS THAT THEY HAVE THE ABILITY TO DO FOR THEMSELVES.

It is important early in recovery that parents receive our vote of confidence in their ability to lead their families. Parents sometimes become dependent on outsiders to address their child's inappropriate or acting-out behavior. It is not unusual for the following cycle to occur:

⇓ Adolescent acts out.

⇓ Parent calls counselor and tells on the adolescent.

⇓ Counselor confronts the adolescent.

⇒ Adolescent changes the behavior.

In this situation, counselors are assuming parental responsibilities. Whenever a counselor does something that parents can do for themselves, they reinforce the parent's message that the parents are incompetent and need intervention to parent their children. It is often easier and sometimes quicker if the counselor addresses the behavior; however, it sabotages the family's recovery process. It is more time consuming but more helpful to work with the parents and teach them to address their child's behavior.

8. BE AWARE OF THE ADOLESCENT'S SENSITIVITY TO CONFLICT WITHIN THE MARITAL DYAD.

If the family system is in relapse, unresolved conflict frequently surfaces between the parents in the system. Adolescents are particularly sensitive to this conflict and the conflict often surfaces the fear in the adolescent that the parents will split up if the conflict continues. At family therapy sessions I have often witnessed parents beginning to argue with one another. During these sessions, the addicted adolescent often does something inappropriate which allows the parents to shift their focus from one another to address the adolescent's behavior. If adolescents are concerned about the conflict, they might consider a relapse as a way to take the focus off the parental conflict and keep the focus on themselves. If I suspect that marital issues will surface during the session, I often exclude adolescents in recovery from that session. This is not done in an attempt to hide the conflict from the adolescent, but is rather an attempt to restore appropriate boundaries to the system. I encourage parents to share with the kids that they do have some issues that they need to work out, but also to inform the kids that this is adult business and will be handled by the adults in the family.

9. DO NOT MAKE THE RECOVERING ADOLESCENT RESPONSIBLE FOR ADDRESSING PARENTAL ALCOHOLISM OR DRUG ADDICTION.

Professionals who work with addicted teens recognize that parental alcoholism and addiction is a problem for a significant number of these families. We struggle with the best way to address this issue with the parents. Because this is a sensitive and difficult issue to address, counselors, as well as non-drinking spouses, often rely on the recovering adolescent to confront the parent's drinking or use. If the goal of early recovery is to re-establish the parents as the head of the household, asking the adolescent to assume responsibility for confronting and intervening upon parental drinking contradicts this goal. Adolescents are encouraged to discuss their feelings about the parent's drinking or use if it is safe for the adolescent to do this in the family environment. However, confronting the use and suggesting an intervention in that use is the responsibility of the counselor and the other adult in the family.

10. PROVIDE FAMILIES WITH EDUCATION ABOUT FAMILY RECOVERY AND FAMILY RELAPSE PREVENTION.

I often use the relapse signs and symptoms discussed in the previous chapter as an educational and monitoring tool for family members. I ask them to identify which of these relapse behaviors they feel will be most relevant to their family system. I also ask them to review periodically how they are doing in regard to sliding into these patterns. When helping families to understand family relapse prevention, it is also important to identify other relapse dynamics that might be particularly relevant and specific to their family system.

11. **TWELVE STEPS FOR PARENTING.**

Introduce the parents to the "Twelve Steps for Parenting" developed by Paul Trussel at the Pennyroyal Center in Hopkinsville, Kentucky. They provide simple and straight forward guidelines designed to help the family meet their early recovery tasks. A copy of these Twelve Steps is included in the appendix of this book.

CONCLUSION

Specialized treatment for adolescent substance abuse is a relatively new clinical phenomenon. We have learned a great deal in the last ten years. I spend a significant portion of every week talking to adolescents. I firmly believe that adolescent use of alcohol and other mood altering substances continues to be a serious problem among our youth. Judging from what adolescents tell me, substance abuse is not on the decline. However, treatment which specifically addresses substance abuse and addictions is becoming less available to our young people.

It is important to keep in mind that adolescents can and do recover from chemical dependency and psychiatric disorders. Adolescents may not recover quickly, easily or as neatly as we would like. Nonetheless, change does happen. It is important that we, the professionals working with them, continue to believe in them and advocate for them to insure that they are able to receive the help they deserve and need. We are responsible for believing in our youth and providing them hope for new beginnings.

A NEW BEGINNING

For most of us, misery and pain were all we knew.
We had a sense of false pride and our lives were through
We did not know we were destined to die
Unless we surrendered and gave up that high
We fought and we struggled and our wound did not mend
Only to discover that this was a beginning, not an end
Our lives are now filled with serenity and love
And our thoughts are uplifting, like the wings of a dove.

Shannon W.
(Recovering Young Person)

APPENDIX

SURVIVING THROUGH THE STEPS:
A PARENTS GUIDE*

Often the world is too much with us. Joy seems far removed, and we reflect on days long past for fond memories to remind us of how it could be today if . . . we look towards the future with despair rather than faith.

Lessons in life as a parent in recent times appear as our worst moments; yet we survive.

Hope is held out to us as a daily reprieve from fear - the fear that our child might continue chemical dependency despite our love, prayers or actions. We are survivors who have bred survivors. Our examples demonstrate faith in the basis for accepting today. If we accept today, survival is assured. There are certain steps which, if willingly used as guide lines, can benefit parents by allowing them to be consistent and positive in dealing with their adolescents. These steps are for the purpose of assisting the parent in maintaining some detachment from their adolescent as well as encouraging the adolescent to assume responsibility for his or her own behavior.

These steps are:

1. We admitted we were powerless over addiction—that trying to control our children's lives makes our own life unmanageable.

2. Always make an effort to show your children how much you care. Communicate that message to them in all interactions, especially when they are having problems.

3. Maintain a positive mental attitude about your ability to be a parent. Trust your instincts and know where you stand.

4. Do not rely on the police or your children's school to be parents. They are unable to care the way you do.

5. Set clear rules and limits for your children. Most do not have the ability to set rules and limits for themselves.

6. Maintain your own supportive relationships. Your children cannot meet your emotional needs, nor can they establish parent-child boundaries.

7. Make sure your home is a safe, secure and positive environment. This includes appropriate privacy for each family member.

8. Follow through with consequences for your children's misbehavior. Make sure the consequences are immediate and related to the misbehavior, not your anger.

9. Do not prevent the natural consequences your children receive for misbehavior outside of the home. They will learn quickly if you let them.

10. Guide your children through life. They will often need help with homework, social situations, future plans, and complex feelings. Never give up trying to direct and redirect their energy.

11. Do not accept responsibility for your children's feelings or the outcome of their decisions. When your children succeed or do poorly it is their reward or consequence, not yours.

12. Your role as a parent is to provide a foundation for a life to be built, and that foundation is strongest with love, direction, and respect. Remember that your children are not less than and no greater than you. As parents these suggestions may seem extraordinary and excessive. We may believe ourselves too busy to use these guides in our daily affairs. It may seem that once again our children have imposed upon us. This thinking will pass as our Higher Power restores us. Our progress will be noticed by others including our children.

** Reprinted with permission of
Paul Trussel of the Penny Royal Center.*

WHEN TREATMENT IS NOT AVAILABLE

One of the key challenges facing many of us who work with young people are the limited resources for indigent clients. Many times we are faced with long waiting lists at public-funded facilities, difficult to treat teens who are not accepted into programs, and a lack of any local resources. We are faced with three key questions: 1) how to increase resources for indigent clients, 2) how to maintain clients in the community while waiting for openings, and 3) how to set up community-based supports for clients who cannot receive care. Although there are no easy or magic answers to these questions, guidelines for addressing these concerns are outlined below.

1. HOW TO INCREASE RESOURCES FOR INDIGENT CLIENTS.

A. There are public-funded facilities and not-for-profit treatment centers throughout the state. These may not be local but may still prove to be valuable resources for your clients. Find out where these facilities are.

B. Visit the facilities and try to develop a relationship with someone at the treatment center. Having a relationship with staff can result in the staff finding a bed for your patient more quickly.

C. There are certain times during the year when census is down and treatment centers are more likely to have openings. Typically, it is easier to find placements for teens during summer months and times around major holidays.

D. Some treatment centers receive funds to serve indigent clients but never seem to have any beds available. If this happens frequently, challenge the center on this.

E. Most insurance supported treatment centers are willing to provide some free care. Pick a center that does quality care and negotiate with them. Many will agree to give your department one free bed for every four or five clients you refer who have insurance.

F. New treatment centers are more likely to give charity beds in an effort to establish themselves in the community.

G. When you are able to find care for an indigent client, choose the client carefully. Choose the client who has the most potential to benefit from the program.

2. **MAINTAINING CLIENTS IN THE COMMUNITY WHILE WAITING FOR A BED.**

A. Try to utilize the time that the teen is waiting to prepare the teen and the family for the inpatient treatment experience.

B. Set up structure for the teen and family. This includes guidelines for school attendance and behavior at home.

C. Require the teen and parents to start attending self-help groups.

D. Establish an abstinence contract with the teen. Expect that the teen will continue to use. This will help break through the teens' denial once they do enter treatment.

E. Have the teen and parents talk to other teens and families who have been through treatment.

F. Clearly outline the consequences of any further drug or alcohol-related incidents.

3. **INCREASING RECOVERY RESOURCES IN THE COMMUNITY.**

A. In communities where resources are limited, net working is essential. Schools, probation departments, community volunteers, and local mental health centers must network together to increase resources.

B. Schools, local community mental health agencies and probation departments can develop drug education and support groups for teens and families.

C. Utilize community volunteers. Recovering individuals are sometimes willing to donate time as part of their recovery program. They are willing to talk to groups of teens and with some training may be willing to facilitate groups.

D. Utilize the AA/NA communities. There are meetings in communities of all sizes that the adolescents can attend. In addition, the recovering community may be willing to hold groups in jail or juvenile detention centers.

E. Network the recovering young people. When adolescents have a place to meet and an opportunity to organize, recovery rates improve. Encourage the teens to develop sober social activities such as softball or bowling teams and sober dances or outings.

F. Find out through networking if there are any recovering teens in your community and utilize them as peer helpers.

HOW TO SELECT THE APPROPRIATE
TREATMENT CENTER

1. Find out what arrangements can be made to accommodate adolescents with limited financial resources (i.e., does the treatment facility accept Medicaid, provide for scholarship care, or receive state funding?) Most treatment centers are willing to offer some free care for individuals with whom they have strong referral relationships.

2. What type of staff to patient ratio does the program have? One therapist for every six patients is a comfortable ratio. The treatment team should also consist of a recreational therapist (one for every twenty patients) and a family therapist. What are the staffing patterns during the weekend and evenings? For each eight patients there should be at least one clinical staff to manage and supervise the milieu.

3. What does the initial assessment consist of, how long does it take and who conducts it? It is not always necessary that the assessment counselor have a Master's degree, but this individual should have a Bachelor's degree and have at least two years of adolescent experience.

4. Find out what percentage of the adolescents assessed at the facility are found to be appropriate for admission to that facility and what percentage are referred elsewhere. If accurate, thorough, and ethical assessments are being done, a significant number of the teens assessed will be referred to outpatient counseling, family counseling or psychiatric services. Be leery of programs that admit all the teens they assess.

5. What are the admission criteria? These criteria should be very specific and describe who gets referred for inpatient vs. outpatient. Do not hesitate to ask why particular recommendations are made.

6. Does the program offer any outpatient services? Providers who offer a continuum of care are usually more conservative in recommending inpatient care. Programs that believe that all teens who are using substances need inpatient care may recommend hospitalizing teens who might be more appropriate for outpatient treatment.

7. How is treatment individualized? What is done for teens with special issues such as cocaine addiction, teens with previous treatment, dual diagnosis? Is the treatment individualized enough to provide for individual and family counseling as well as group?

8. What type of aftercare is provided and what is the cost? Effective aftercare services include the family and are intensive (i.e., offering group sessions as well as skill building, recreational activities and psychoeducational groups.)

9. What is the program's policy on working with adolescents who have conduct disorders and behavior problems? If programs are not prepared to work with teens who present behavioral problems, it is better to determine this in the beginning and refer the teen to another program.

10. What type of qualifications do the staff have? Is there a combination of experience, academic training and staff who are recovering? Young staff provide enthusiasm, experienced staff provide wisdom, recovering staff provide hope, and educated staff provide clinical sophistication. The best treatment teams provide a combination of these characteristics.

11. What is the treatment schedule and staff coverage for evenings and weekends? The busier the schedule the better. Structured treatment activities should be scheduled seven days a week. Treatment does not stop at 5:00 p.m.

12. What does the program offer for families? The families need support groups, education groups, and family counseling sessions.

13. What is the length of the program and what are the total costs? Clinically sophisticated programs are moving toward variable lengths of stay based on patient needs.

14. What is the involvement of the medical director, psychologist, and psychiatrist? What type of psychological testing is done? Given the complexity of addicted teens, some type of psychological screening is essential for all teens during treatment.

15. How is school involved in the program and how closely does the treatment center work with the home school upon discharge? It is critical to get a realistic and clear understanding of what can and cannot be accomplished during the school programs. If the adolescent attends school only two hours a day while in treatment, the adolescent will likely fall behind in school. The teen, the family, the school, and the referent need to be prepared for this in order to plan for a smooth transition back into the community.

16. Does the program include involvement in AA and/or NA and do the adolescents have an opportunity to attend meetings outside the treatment center? AA and NA exposure is critical. The more exposure teens have to these programs during treatment, the more likely they will continue their involvement with these programs following discharge. Programs that utilize AA/NA volunteers have more success in selling the teens on the concept of self-help programs.

17. What type of behavior management system does the program have and how are behavior problems addressed? A structured and consistent approach to managing patient behavior is important.

18. What does the program do to help the adolescent and family prepare for re-entry? Make sure you let the facility know that you want to be closely involved in this process.

19. How long has the program been providing services for addicted teens? There is no substitute for experience when it comes to working successfully with teens.

20. Become familiar with what type of teens do well in what programs and refer accordingly. No program can meet the needs of all adolescents. For instance, you may discover that some programs provide excellent services to males, but have limited success with females.

21. Visit the treatment center and meet the staff. Judge for yourself what kind of atmosphere and attitude prevails. Is the center clean and comfortable? Do the staff project a positive attitude toward recovery and a nurturing attitude toward the patients? Are the patients engaged in the recovery process? Are the patients and staff working together vs. engaging in power struggles.

22. Maintain a realistic attitude about adolescent recovery. Adolescents will struggle and slip following treatment. Slips can be part of the recovery process, they can also be detours, but they do not have to be the end of the road. It is unrealistic to expect treatment to change the teen and the family completely. There are some excellent treatment programs. Successful treatment is evidenced by how well the treatment center works with the teen, the family, and the community to assist the adolescent in continuing in recovery after making mistakes.

Janice Gabe, MSW, CADAC,
New Perspectives of Indiana, Inc.

TWELVE STEPS FOR ADOLESCENTS

1. We admitted we were powerless over alcohol—that our lives had become unmanageable.
   Admitted that when we participate in drinking, drugging, and acting out behavior that our lives get out of control.

2. Came to believe a Power greater than ourselves could restore us to sanity.
   Came to believe that we could change with the help of others.

3. Made a decision to turn our will and our lives over to the care of God as we understood Him.
   Made a decision to work with others to make changes in our behavior and our value system.

4. Made a searching and fearless moral inventory of ourselves.
   Made a list of behaviors we need to change and recognized the positive strengths we have that will help us make these changes.

5. Admitted to God, to ourselves and to another human being the exact nature of our wrongs.
   Shared our list with another person.

6. Were entirely ready to have God remove all these defects of character.
   Were ready to leave these old behaviors, attitudes, and values behind.

7. Humbly asked God to remove our shortcomings.
   Became willing to work with others to change these old behaviors, attitudes and values.

8. Made a list of all the persons we had harmed, and became willing to make amends to them all.
   Made a list of people, including myself, who have been hurt by our behavior and decided to make amends to them.

9. Made direct amends to such people whenever possible except when to do so would injure them or others.
   Took responsibility for our behavior and for forgiving ourselves by making amends to people who have been hurt by our behavior.

10. Continued to take personal inventory and when we were wrong promptly admitted it.
    Continue to take responsibility for ourselves and admit when we are wrong.

11. Sought through prayer and meditation to improve our conscious contact with God as we understood Him, praying only for knowledge of His will for us and the power to carry that out.
    Tried, with the help of others, to be a better person—someone we can be proud of and live with.

12. Having had a spiritual awakening as a result of these steps, we tried to carry this message to alcoholics and practice these principles in all of our affairs.
    Having been able to change our lives with the help of others, we offer our help to others.

Alcoholics Anonymous, Alcoholics Anonymous World Service, Inc., New York City, 1976.

Suggestions for interpreting The Twelve Steps for Adolescents.
This is particularly helpful for teens with multiple problems.

Copyright Janice Gabe, 1992.
This material cannot be reproduced without the written consent of Janice Gabe.

BIBLIOGRAPHY

Bell, Tammy L. Preventing Adolescent Relapse: A Guide for Parents, Teachers and Counselors. Independence, MO: Herald House/Independence Press, 1990.

Benard, Bonnie. Fostering Resiliency in Kids: Protective Factors in the Family, School, and Community. Oak Brook, IL: Distributed by the Midwest Regional Center for Drug-Free Schools and Communities, 1991.

Cavaiola, Allen and Carolann Caine-Cavaiola. "Basics of Adolescent Development for the Chemical Dependency Professional." Journal of Chemical Dependency Treatment, Vol. 2, no. 1. (1988/89): 11-23.

Gabe, Janice E. "Adolescent Co-dependency." The Counselor Magazine (March/April 1990): 20-23.

A Professional's Guide to Adolescent Substance Abuse. Springfield,IL: Academy of Addictions Treatment Professionals, 1989.

"Depression: Avoiding a Roadblock to Teenage Recovery." Addiction and Recovery Magazine, Vol. 12, no. 1 (January/February, 1992): 17-19.

"Twenty-one Points to Consider in Seeking an Adolescent Treatment Center." Adolescent Counselor Magazine (December 1990/January 1991): 26-28.

Gorski, Terence, T. and Merlene Miller. Staying Sober—A Guide for Relapse Prevention. Independence, MO: Herald House/Independence Press, 1986.

Harrison, Patricia Ann and Norman G. Hoffman. "Adolescent Residential Treatment Intake and Follow-up Findings." CATOR Report, 1987.

McIntyre, Kevin, Douglas White, and Richard Yoast. Resilience Among High Risk Youth. Madison, WI: Wisconsin Clearinghouse, 1990.

Mercer, Joyce. Behind the Mask of Adolescent Satanism. Minneapolis, MN: Deaconess Press, 1991.

Schneidman, E. S. Definition of Suicide. New York: John Wiley and Sons, Inc., 1981.

Terro Mooney, Belinda. Leave Me Alone! - Helping Your Troubled Teenager. Summit, PA: Tab Books, 1993.

White, William L. The Culture of Addiction/The Culture of Recovery, Books 1 and 2. Bloomington, IL: The Lighthouse Training Institute, 1990.

ORDER FORM

Professional Resource Publication
P.O. Box 501485
Indianapolis, Indiana 46256

Books available by this author:

❑ Please send me _____ copies of *A Professionals Guide to Dual Disorders in Adolescents* at **$17.00** per copy.

❑ Please send me _____ copies of *Cultures of Change: Recovery and Relapse Prevention for Dually Diagnosed and Addicted Adolescents* at **$12.95** per copy.

Send to:

Name_____

Address _____

_____

City_____ST____Zip _____

Phone _____

Shipping:

Book Rate: $2.00 for the first book and 75¢ for each additional book.

Airmail: $3.50 per book

Sales Tax:

Please add 5% tax for books shipped to Indiana addresses. (85¢ for $17.00 purchase and 65¢ for $12.95 purchase).